Witnessing —

A Lifestyle

Kay L. Meyer

"Go therefore and make disciples of all the nations, baptizing them in the name of the Father and the Son and the Holy Spirit, teaching them to observe all that I commanded you; and lo, I am with you always, even to the end of the age" (Matthew 28:19-20).

Published by
Family Shield Ministries, Inc.
P. O. Box 230015
St. Louis, MO 63123

Witnessing—A Lifestyle
Kay L. Meyer

Library of Congress Cataloging-in-Publication Data
Library of Congress Control Number: 2008907403

Meyer, Kay L.
  Witnessing—A Lifestyle
  ISBN-13: 978-0-9744536-1-3
  ISBN-10: 0-9744536-1-7

For more information, contact:

Family Shield Ministries, Inc.
P. O. Box 230015
St. Louis, Missouri 63123
(314) 772-6070 or (866) 370-6070
www.familyshieldministries.com

Thank You!

A SPECIAL THANK YOU TO NORTHERN ILLINOIS DISTRICT LWML WOMEN

The women of the Northern Illinois District (NID) of the Lutheran Women's Missionary League (LWML) approved a grant to help Family Shield Ministries produce this resource. Rev. Roger Sonnenberg, chairman of Family Shield Ministries recently shared, "The women of LWML are always looking for ways to share the Gospel. They do this in my own congregation in Arcadia, California and they do it in the Northern Illinois District of the LWML. Thank you, women of the Lutheran Women's Missionary League! You are special!"

ACKNOWLEDGEMENTS

I want to thank my husband, Tjaden, for his continued support, prayers, and partnership in the Gospel. He has always made the Lord and our family his highest priorities.

And, I also want to thank Dianne Sudbrock of The Write Design. She was the graphic designer and editor for the project. She offered her suggestions and professional expertise. Finally, I want to thank Martha Jander who did the final editing. Without all these individual's support and assistance the book would not have been produced.

WITNESSING—A LIFESTYLE

Contents

Part 4—Witnessing in the Community, Congregations and Schools

What Is Witnessing? How Do I Go About Sharing My Faith?

If you're like I am, your congregation or denomination talks a lot about evangelism and witnessing, but doesn't offer much assistance in training Christians how to share God's love in their daily lives with family members and friends.

Sharing our faith isn't difficult. It can happen naturally as we talk about life issues with family members, friends, and those we meet in our daily life.

I frequently teach workshops and Bible studies on the topic of "Witnessing—A Lifestyle." Some of the points I discuss in these presentations include:
- Begin with prayer.
- Build a relationship.
- Share a personal testimony and relate faith to life issues.
- Listen, show concern, and respond to needs.
- Share the Law and Gospel.

Remember, this book discusses lifestyle evangelism. You do not need to tell those you meet everything you know at once. Move slowly. If you know them, you will see them again. Build trusting relationships.

Some evangelism programs like to give you specific questions that you should use in sharing Christ. *Dialogue Evangelism* is like this. James D. Kennedy introduced this evangelism program that is still used today by many congregations. I participated in this program at my former congregation and went out on evangelism calls using this program for over 15 years.

I was a trainer for the *Dialogue Evangelism* program for three years. This book is different. It encourages Christians to rely upon the Lord and His Spirit for guidance. There is not just one way to share the Gospel. There are many ways to do it. We do not give you a specific question or series of questions that you must use when you witness. Instead, we encourage you to pray and rely upon the Holy Spirit to guide and direct your discussions with those you know.

The articles assembled in this book were written over a period of 13 years and were originally published in "The Great Commission" column of the *St. Louis Metro Voice* newspaper. My prayer is that this book will encourage and equip you as you talk about the Lord with family, friends, and those you meet in your community.

Part 1

Witnessing Basics

"The harvest is plentiful, but the workers are few. There-fore beseech the Lord of the harvest to send out workers into His harvest" (Matthew 9:37-38).

Build a Relationship — Then Witness

Witnessing to those who are not Christians is not always easy, but all Christians are called to be witnesses. Just as Christ shared God's love in a myriad of ways, so can we.

Consider some of the following non-threatening ways you might share your faith with unbelievers or those who have fallen away from the church. Start by building a relationship with those you come in contact with on a daily basis — then wait on the Lord to open doors and give you the words to speak of His love.

1. Begin with prayer. Ask the Lord to open doors for your witness of Christ. Pray that He will give you the words to speak in the hour that you need them. Pray by name for those you know who don't know Christ.

2. Offer to pray for a friend who is experiencing problems. Better yet, offer to pray with them. Find an empty office or room and pray together about the problem he or she is experiencing.

3. Send a get-well or sympathy card. Write an appropriate Bible verse on it.

4. Write to relatives and friends who live out of town and share your faith. Send a letter to your children or grandchildren away at col-

lege and share your faith with them through a letter. E-mails are also appropriate.

5. Purchase several different Christian tracts and enclose one within bills and special occasion cards. Or, give scriptural plastic pocket cards to friends and acquaintances going through trials or difficulties.

6. Take a bowl of soup or batch of cookies to a sick neighbor, then stay and visit with them. Or telephone someone who has recently lost a loved one and spend time listening to their concerns.

7. Instead of drinking coffee on your office break, invite an unchurched co-worker to take a daily walk with you and build a relationship of trust and respect.

8. Offer to teach a home Bible study and invite an unchurched friend or neighbor to join your group.

9. Invite a friend or acquaintance to a prayer breakfast, potluck, or special event at your congregation.

10. Organize a special evangelism event for your congregation such as a friendship festival.

11. Wear a Christian cross or Christian pin. Wearing Christian symbols often causes people to ask, "What does that pin mean?" This can often open a door to share your faith.

12. Offer to baby-sit for members of your evangelism board, for your pastor's new member classes, or for a young single parent while she shops on a Saturday morning or afternoon.

13. Organize a support group for single parents at your congregation, or for grandparents raising their grandchildren.

14. Purchase an audio-cassette of a Christian radio program that you think friends would enjoy and share it with them, or purchase a Christian book or Bible for them.

Thousands of people don't know Christ. How many do you speak with each day on the job, in your neighborhood, or within your own family? Discover other simple non-threatening ways to witness. Then when the Lord opens the door of opportunity, speak the precious words of the Gospel. *"I am not ashamed of the gospel, for it is the power of God for salvation to everyone who believes, to the Jew first and also to the Greek. For in it the righteousness of God is revealed from faith to faith; as it is written, 'But the righteous man shall live by faith'" (Romans 1:16-17).* Why not build a relationship—then witness about His love?

Begin with Prayer

A Christian man recognized the importance of prayer in bringing people to Jesus as their Savior and Lord. He selected three friends who were not Christians and began praying for their salvation.

The first man came to faith in Christ after three years. The second friend came to faith after 10 years. The Christian continued praying for the third friend. When the Christian was 58 years old he died. He had prayed for his friend for 35 years. Three years after the man joined his Savior in heaven, the man he had been praying for placed his faith in the Lord. God answers prayers. He desires that we pray for the unsaved.

Do you know family, friends, co-workers, neigh-bors, or acquaintances who don't know Christ as their Savior and Lord? Have you prayed for any of them this week?

Although we know we should pray for spiritual issues, our busy lives, complicated by Satan's schemes (Ephesians 6:11-12), often keep us from prayer. Do you desire to be used by God to help people hear the Gospel message of grace through faith in Christ Jesus? Then begin with prayer.

Pray for workers within God's Kingdom. Jesus said to His disciples, *"The harvest is plentiful, but the workers are few. Therefore beseech the Lord of the harvest to send out workers into His harvest" (Matthew 9:37-38).*

Be specific in your prayer request. Ask God to open hearts to hear the Gospel. Listen to needs and concerns. Be willing to lend a helping hand and/or witness as the Lord leads.

Be persistent in prayer. Be patient. Learn to wait upon the Lord to open doors. Remember, God's timing is not always our timing. Some people tend to move ahead of the Holy Spirit. At times, well-meaning

Christians decide they must witness. Rather than beginning with prayer and waiting upon the Lord to open doors of opportunity, they bulldoze their way into people's lives. They forget the Holy Spirit needs to prepare hearts in advance.

The Bible talks about three different forms for prayer: independent or private prayer (Matthew 6:6-7), small group prayer (Matthew 18:20), and corporate or large group prayer (Acts 12:5). Although as Christians we often use independent prayer and corporate prayer, we don't always use small group prayer. A small group may be your family gathered around the dinner table; or it might be an intimate group of believers gathered together in a home, at a restaurant, or within the church. As you pray for those who don't know Christ, try to include all three types of prayer.

Prayer can also be used to open doors to share the Gospel message. Often when listening to someone's family or work problems, we say, "I'll pray for you." Consider saying instead, "May I pray with you?" Then find an empty office or quiet corner and pray with them. Include the Gospel in your prayer. Thank and praise God the Father for sending His only begotten Son into the world, for the sacrifice Christ made for our sins, for the joy and forgiveness that is ours through faith in Christ, and for the free gift of eternal life. We can use prayers to communicate the Gospel message in a non-threatening way. The following story will illustrate how this can happen.

> Consider saying instead, "May I pray with you?" Then find an empty office or quiet corner and pray with them.

My neighbor was depressed. She came to visit. I listened to her problems, then offered to pray with her. At least once a week she returned for another visit. She always asked me to pray with her. I asked God to heal her and bless her family. As I prayed, I included the Gospel message.

Several weeks later, right after we had prayed, she stated, "I've always thought that if I was a good person, God would accept me and grant me eternal life, but you said it is only through Christ's righteousness that we obtain eternal life in heaven. You said Jesus took my sins upon Himself on the cross. How can Jesus take my sins? How can I take His righteousness? I don't understand. Would you explain it to me?"

She had asked a question. Questions are often open doors from the Lord, and God granted me the words to answer her questions, as He had promised in Matthew 10:19.

Sometimes prayer is the only way we can reach unchurched or fallen-away Christians. A Christian grandmother shared recently, "My son was raised in a Christian home, but now he never attends church. He seems angry at God and has no interest in God's Word. Worst of all, he doesn't allow our two grandchildren to attend Sunday school or church. It grieves Bill and me so! We try to witness to him, but when we talk to him about his relationship with the Lord, he just gets angry. What should we do?"

We prayed together for her son. I encouraged this woman not only to ask, but to begin seeking and knocking on God's door for her son and grandchildren (Matthew 7:7). Although she and her husband had been praying privately about this situation, they had not shared their concern with other Christians. They are now requesting specific prayers for Bill and his two children. Would you pray that God will bring someone into Bill's life who will witness to him? And pray that he will allow his children to learn about Jesus.

Another story. This one involves a couple who are Jehovah's Witnesses. I witnessed to them off and on over a period of six years. Because of my work in cult evangelism, especially to Jehovah's Witnesses, this couple will literally no longer speak to me. I can no longer witness to them, but I can pray. And I do!

God desires all to be saved. The Bible states, *"First of all, then, I urge that entreaties and prayers, petitions and thanksgivings, be made on behalf of all men, for kings and all who are in authority, so that we may lead a tranquil and quiet life in all godliness and dignity. This is good and acceptable in the sight of God our Savior, who desires all men to be saved and to come to the knowledge of the truth. For there is one God, and one mediator also between God and men, the man Jesus Christ, who gave Himself as ransom for all" (1 Timothy 2:1-6).* Because I know it is God's will for all to come to the knowledge of the Son, I continued to pray for this couple. I have committed them into God's hands.

I'd like to invite you to pray for those you know who are not Christians. Maybe the Lord has brought to your mind several individuals you know who don't know the Lord. Would you select at least one to pray for now?

Lord, _____ doesn't know you as his/her Savior and Lord.

Open a door for him/her to hear and comprehend the saving Gospel message of God's love through Jesus Christ. Then guide him/her, by Your Spirit, to place his/her trust in You. If it is Your will, use me to witness to _____. In Jesus' name. Amen.

How to Introduce Someone to Christ

The door has opened. You have built a relationship with your friend and now he or she has asked you to explain more about the Christian faith.

You've done your homework and already know your friend did not grow up in the church and he/she knows almost nothing about God, His Word, Jesus, or what it means to have faith in Christ. What key points should you discuss so that your friend hears and understands what it means to be a Christian?

1. **Talk about God.** You might begin by sharing some of God's attributes or characteristics. Two attributes that are important to clarify when we share the Gospel are that God is both just and righteous (Psalm 7:11; Daniel 9:14; Matthew 5:48). He is also loving (John 3:16). Because He is just and righteous He must punish sin. Yet because He loves us He doesn't want us to go to hell.

2. **Talk about Humankind.** Although God created human beings in His image (Genesis 1:26) without sin, they rebelled against God. Satan tempted Eve, then Eve tempted Adam. That one sin of disobedience was passed on to all of us. Sin separates us from God (Romans 5:19a). People cannot save themselves by doing good works (Ephesians 2:8-9; Titus 3:5a).

3. **Talk about sin.** Most people have no trouble talking about God, faith, or Jesus Christ, but sin is another matter. They don't like to be reminded of their sins. When I share the Gospel, I've found it helps to use myself as an example, rather than them. I'll say, "The First Commandment says, 'Love the Lord your God and put Him first.' But, sometimes instead of listening to the sermon and putting God first, my mind wanders and I'm thinking of what I have

to do at home or what I'll be preparing for dinner. It's difficult to put God first all the time, don't you think? Can you think of a time when you haven't put God first?"

It's easy to look at others and see their sin, but it is more difficult to look at ourselves and talk about our sin. The Bible says, *"There is none righteous, not even one; There is none who understands, there is none who seeks for God; All have turned aside, together they have become useless; there is none who does good, there is not even one" (Romans 3:10-12).* And *"for all have sinned and fall short of the glory of God" (Romans 3:23).*

It is imperative that people recognize they are sinners and can't save themselves. Until they understand their sinful nature and sins against God, they cannot see the need for a Savior. Rather than comparing ourselves to other sinners, we need to compare ourselves to Jesus, who is perfectly righteous and holy.

The Law helps us become aware of our sin (Romans 3:20b). God gave us the Ten Commandments to help us see our sins. It is like a mirror. The Law can also be a guide for living. The Ten Commandments tell us how God would like us to live. It shows how we have missed the mark and gone astray. (When we fail, which we will, we know we have a Savior who kept the Law perfectly for us.)

In fact, if we stumble at just one point we become guilty of breaking all of God's Law (James 2:10). Sin separates us from God (Isaiah 59:2), and His justice demands our eternal death (Romans 6:23a).

4. **Talk about Jesus.** Out of great love God the Father sent His only begotten Son from His heavenly home to earth to live the life we are unable to live. Jesus was perfect and righteous. We can't live a perfect life. Jesus did it for us. He then suffered for our sins and was put to death on the cross to satisfy the wages of sin which is death. All our sins were laid on Jesus and He suffered death for us. He rose to life again, conquering death, becoming God's guarantee

of forgiveness and eternal life (Romans 4:24-25).

Talk about who Jesus is and what He did for us. He is both true God and true man (John 1:1, 14; John 20:28; Philippians 2:6). He had to be so that He could take our place and fulfill all God's requirements perfectly. Because Jesus did it, we can trust that it is sufficient.

5. **Talk about repentance.** God tells us to repent of our sins. He wants us to be sorry that we have sinned against Him and to turn away from our sins. He wants us to turn to Him and trust Him for our salvation and life (Luke 13:3; Acts 17:30).

6. **Talk about faith.** How do we get all that God did for us in Christ? How do we internalize it so it becomes our own? Through faith! Faith is not only knowledge of what God has done in Christ. It says "Yes" to it all, and above all, trusts in what God did in Christ. Faith is primarily trusting in Christ's life, death, and resurrection for our salvation.

    Want to do more studying about faith? Here are some places in the Bible to review: Luke 17:6; John 3:16,36; 5:24; 11:25; Hebrews 11:1-3 (a definition of faith).

    Faith is a free gift of God (Ephesians 2:8-9). When we freely receive faith in Christ, He forgives all our sins and grants us eternal life. When we have faith, eternal life is now a present reality!

7. **Talk about the gift of eternal life.** Trusting in Christ, God saves us and gives us eternal life. Eternal life is also a free gift of God and is not dependent upon what we do (Ephesians 2:8-9).

Acts 16:23-34 gives us a Biblical example for us to consider: The jailer at Philippi asked Paul and Silas, *"'Sirs, what must I do to be saved?' They said, 'Believe in the Lord Jesus, and you will be saved, you and your household'"* (Acts 16:30-31).

Please note that YOU do not need to do anything toward being saved BUT believe in Jesus Christ! Ask the persons you are talking to if they understand what you've shared and if they have any questions. Then ask them if they repent of their sins and believe in Christ. Tell them they don't need to understand everything about God before they place their faith in Christ.

Explain that when they profess faith, the Holy Spirit has given them that faith through the message just shared (1 Corinthians 2:4-5), and has come into their hearts. He will teach them all things.

Pray together, if possible. Invite them to study the Bible and attend church with you. As you pray, thank God for what He has done and ask Him to keep them in faith.

Sometimes those we speak with may listen attentively, but are not led to place their faith in Christ. Remember, it is not our job to make people Christians. The Holy Spirit brings people to faith. Do share the message of salvation. Then, leave the rest in God's hands.

Use Prayer and Every Opportunity to Share Christ

"God, please take Nana to heaven to be with you. Help her remember all the Bible verses she learned over the years and give her a peaceful release into your Kingdom." This was one of my prayers some years ago. My husband's 104-year old grandmother lived in her own home until she was 98 years old. Six years before her death she moved into a nursing home. It had been six years of pain and suffering. God finally answered my prayer and took Nana to be with Him on March 8, 1996.

Our family rejoices that she knew the Lord and is in heaven with Him. Hours after her death I was on the phone with my pastor, "Nana's grand-daughter from New York will be traveling in for the funeral. She isn't a Christian. We'd like to use this time to witness to her and others who attend the funeral parlor and memorial service. Will you share the Gospel during the memorial service?"

Nana's funeral and conversations about her death gave me many opportunities to share my faith. We told people of the joy we were experiencing knowing that she was in heaven. A co-worker said, "Wow, she was in the nursing home for six years and suffered so much. She deserves to go to heaven!"

I responded, "Suffering doesn't gain us eternal life. Nana's in heaven because she believed in Christ. She wasn't perfect, only forgiven."

When my 18-year-old son got home from school on the afternoon she died I said, "Jeff, Nana died today. Yes, we'll miss her. But, just think of the happy reunion that's going on in heaven today! She's seeing her Savior for the first time. And she has joined her mother and father, all eight of her brothers and sisters, her two daughters, and one of her grandsons."

Are you using prayer and every opportunity to share your faith in Christ? If not, why not?

Prayer is so vital to our faith. It links us to God and His power. How would you rate your prayer life? ☐ Weak ☐ Average ☐ Excellent. If you're like most of us, your prayer life probably needs some improvement.

Let's review some facts from God's Word concerning prayer. We know that God the Father hears our prayers because of Christ. The Bible says, *"... for through Him [Jesus] we both have our access in one Spirit to the Father" (Ephesians 2:18)*. We know God wants us to be persistent in prayer. *"Ask, and it will be given to you; seek, and you will find; knock, and it will be opened to you" (Matthew 7:7)*. We know Christians pray for themselves, their families, and others. *"Be anxious for nothing, but in everything by prayer and supplication with thanksgiving let your request be made known to God" (Philippians 4:6)*. *"With all prayer and petition pray at all times in the Spirit, and with this in view, be on the alert with all perseverance and petition for all the saints" (Ephesians 6:18)*. We know God always answers the prayers of His people. He doesn't always answer "Yes." Sometimes He answers, "No" or "Wait."

> Are you using prayer and every opportunity to share your faith in Christ? If not, why not?

Want to improve your prayer life? Here are some suggestions to consider. Pray privately. Get up early and spend time alone with the Lord in prayer. Pray together in small groups. Pray with your spouse and/or children every morning before you leave for school or work. Begin a prayer group at your office or church. Learn about prayer resources that are available by visiting your local Christian bookstore. Read a book on prayer or listen to an audiocassette about prayer. Join your congregation's prayer chain. Organize a prayer vigil.

Be specific in your prayer request. When you are specific you often see how God is answering the prayer. Consider writing your prayers down. This can help you concentrate. It also gives you a record to review God's answers.

Seek to know God's will. *"For this reason also, since the day we heard of it* [the faith of a believer] *we have not ceased to pray for you and to ask that you may be filled with the knowledge of His will in all spiritual wisdom and understanding"* (Colossians 1:9). Why were they praying? *"So that you may walk in a manner worthy of the Lord, to please Him in all respects, bearing fruit in every good work and increasing in the knowledge of God"* (Colossians 1:10).

Opportunities to pray and grow in your knowledge of prayer abound. Use prayer opportunities. Why not gather with others to pray for our country, families, children, congregations, and community on the National Day of Prayer?

As you pray and share your faith, be aware that God's Word says there are obstacles to prayer. Knowing these could help you when opportunities to witness arise. Some obstacles include:

1) Willful disobedience before God. *"Then you returned and wept before the Lord; but the Lord did not listen to your voice nor give ear to you"* (Deuteronomy 1:45). Why didn't the Lord listen? Because they rebelled against God's commands. *"He who turns away his ear from listening to the law, Even his prayer is an abomination"* (Proverbs 28:9).

2) Unrepented sin. *"If I regard wickedness in my heart, the Lord will not hear"* (Psalm 66:18). *"So when you spread out your hands in prayer, I will hide my eyes from you; Yes, even though you multiply prayers, I will not listen. Your hands are covered with blood"* (Isaiah 1:15). *"But your iniquities have made a separation between you and your God, And your sins have hidden His face from you, so that He does not hear"* (Isaiah 59:2).

3) Unbelief. *"Jesus said..., 'I am the way, and the truth, and the life: no one comes to the Father but through Me"* (John 14:6). *"But he must ask in faith without any doubting, for the one who doubts is like the surf of the sea driven and tossed by the wind. For that man ought not to expect that he will receive anything from the Lord"* (James 1:6-8).

4) Wrong Motive. *"You ask and do not receive, because you ask with wrong motives"* (James 4:3).

Are you or those you are witnessing to rebelling against God's commands, yet still asking God to bless you? Do you have unrepented sin blocking your communication with the Father? Are you doubting God's power? Are you praying with the wrong motives?

What do you do if you realize some of the obstacles apply in your life or in the life of those you are witnessing to? Hear the message of salvation. Place your faith in the One who died and rose for you. Then regularly confess your sins and receive His forgiveness!

For the Bible states, *"First of all, then, I urge that entreaties and prayers, petitions and thanksgivings, be made on behalf of all men, for kings and all who are in authority, so that we may lead a tranquil and quiet life in all godliness and dignity. This is good and acceptable in the sight of God our Savior, who desires all men to be saved and to come to the knowledge of the truth. For there is one God, and one mediator also between God and men, the man Christ Jesus, who gave Himself as a ransom for all"* (1 Timothy 2:1-6).

Using Prayer in Witnessing

"Marcia, you were involved in the New Age Movement prior to becoming a Christian. Can you tell our listeners how you came to faith in Christ?"

In March of 2002 I scheduled a *Family Shield* radio interview with two experts on "Wicca, Witchcraft, and Neopaganism" and planned to spend the entire program discussing this topic. But, God had other plans. First, the engineer was unable to get us connected with the second guest. Then, during my introduction, I asked Marcia how she came to know Christ.

Marcia Montenegro, Director of Christian Answers for the New Age, shared, "Yes, that's correct. I was heavily involved in astrology and the New Age Movement at the time. Then, all of a sudden, out of the blue, I had a compulsion to go to a Christian church."

I asked, "Had someone witnessed to you?"

Marcia said:

No. No one witnessed to me. I just had a compulsion to go

to a Christian church. I didn't want to go. I tried to ignore the compulsion. I thought, at first, the desire came from a previous life. At the time I believed in reincarnation.

Finally, I went to a large church in my community. The first Sunday there was a procession from the back of the church that included the pastors, the choir, and others who would be part of the service. A young boy carrying a cross led it. When that cross passed by me I felt what I call a 'waterfall of love.' I knew it was from God. Not the god of the New Age, but the real God. I began going to church each week after that.

The church I selected was liberal. Rather than proclaiming the Gospel, the pastor preached about current events. I really don't remember hearing the Gospel from the pulpit. I was, however, drawn to the liturgy. It spoke of Christ as the Savior from sin. I was also drawn to the prayers and anytime the liturgy, the prayers, or the Scripture lessons spoke of Christ.

I began attending a Bible study. Later I found out it was a group of individuals who were going to join the church! When I told individuals at the church and in the Bible study that I was an Astrologer, no one seemed to see a problem with it. No one ever told me it was against God's Word.

Finally, without anyone telling me astrology was something God's Word condemns, I decided God didn't like astrology. I thought He wanted me to stop working in astrology. Astrology, at this time, was the focus on my life. I had become well-known for my work and had worked in this area for over 10 years. I had written for national magazines, had spoken at national conventions, and had many clients. So to give it up was a drastic decision. But that's exactly what I did.

It was after I gave up Astrology that I began reading the Bible at home. I began with Matthew. I read Matthew 8. The disciples woke Jesus up because of the storm. Jesus rebuked the storm and His disciples for their lack of faith. I read these verses over and over. It was at this point that God opened my eyes to the truth. I realized that Jesus was true God and true man. I realized He was my Savior. I had been going away from God, studying Eastern religions, involved in Astrology, but now I realized that Jesus had died for me. And I knew I needed a Savior. When I placed my faith in Christ, I knew the Holy Spirit had come to live in me!

> When I placed my faith in Christ, I knew the Holy Spirit had come to live in me!

Throughout the interview, I kept asking questions that would help me understand why the Holy Spirit had begun working in her life, drawn her to attend church, into the Bible, and ultimately to place her faith in Christ! Marcia continued to state, "No one witnessed to me. I seldom heard the Gospel proclaimed at the worship services in this liberal church."

I think at this point I said, "God can even use liberal churches! He certainly did in this case."

Twenty-five minutes of the program had gone by and the break was upon us. It was then that Marcia stated, "I need to add one more thing to my testimony. About four months after I placed my faith in Christ I learned a young Christian man I had met when I was heavily involved in Astrology had decided to pray for me. He had asked others in his prayer group and church to pray for me, too. They had prayed regularly for me during all those months!"

The Holy Spirit had begun working in Marcia's life, had drawn Marcia to attend church and eventually place her faith in Christ because Christians had been praying. The compulsion she had experienced was the urging of the Holy Spirit. Don't forget the importance of prayer in your witnessing efforts. Prayer is powerful, because God is the one who answers prayers!

Ask, and it will be given to you; seek, and you will find; knock, and it will be opened to you. For everyone who asks receives, and he who seeks finds, and to him who knocks, it will be opened" (Matthew 7:7-8).

Do you know people who don't know Christ? Are you wondering how to begin witnessing to them? Begin with prayer! To learn what God's Word has to say about Astrology, read Deuteronomy 18:10-12 and Isaiah 47:12-15.

Prayer—A Vital Part of Ministry

Peter, the apostle, was in prison for preaching Christ. He was bound in chains and guarded by four squads of soldiers. Things looked hopeless, but fervent prayer for him was being made by the church of God (Acts 12:5). Peter escaped from prison in a miraculous way, following the church's fervent prayer. When he arrived at the house of Mary, the mother of John Mark, he found many gathered together praying. God answered the prayers of the early church.

He also answers our prayers today. Although congregations utilize prayer during worship services, some have concerns about the lukewarmness concerning prayer among its members. Concerns include:

- Prayer is often seen as the last resort, rather than a first priority when problems occur.
- Prayer is seen as women's work. Most prayer chains are composed of women, not men.
- Many prayer chains focus on physical, rather than spiritual needs.
- Many members do not know how to pray, or they feel uncomfortable praying out loud.

How do we motivate church members to make prayer a priority? How can we improve congregational prayer life? First and foremost, we focus on the Savior, who died for our sins, and the Gospel, which motivates us to pray. Then we use His Word as our guide and pray for His guidance.

Pray individually (Matthew 6:6-7). Pray together in small groups (Matthew 18:20). Pray corporately during worship services, Bible studies, and at church meetings (Acts 12:3-12).

"Pastors must be role models and teach their members to pray," stated Rev. James Kirk. Rev. Kirk frequently presents prayer workshops, leads a weekly pastors' prayer group, and teaches his members, both young and old, how to pray. "Prayer," he stated, "is one of our congregation's focal points. Just as early apostles devoted themselves to prayer and the ministry of the Word, so must leaders today."

"God has answered so many of my prayers!" said Pauline Miller, who has served on the LCMS Pacific Southwest District Prayer Task Force and frequently presents workshops on prayer. "My pastor asked our prayer group to take the names of several inactive members and pray for them on a regular basis. Shortly after I began praying, one of the women I'd been praying for was at Sunday morning worship service. Today she remains an active member. God answered my prayer!"

The following information was gathered from my interviews with a variety of congregational leaders (pastors, church leaders, and lay members). I hope this information will motivate you to focus more on effective prayer within your congregation.

The prayer chain is the most popular form of prayer ministry within most LCMS congregations. Redeemer Lutheran Church in Thousand Oaks, California, has six prayer chains involving 45-50 members. Rev Elroi Reimnitz said, "Members are only asked to be on the prayer chain for one year. Each year we hold a commissioning worship service. Prayer chain members come to the altar to make their commitment to the Lord."

"We make telephone calls every week and strive to put individuals on the chains who share common interests," remarked Lois Koeshe, one of the three prayer coordinators for Redeemer Lutheran. "One chain is composed of choir members, another is composed of members who are in the sewing group, another is young mothers, and others have individuals who work. Prayer requests are collected each week during the worship service. We also have a prayer container in which people can drop their requests following the service."

The previous week's requests included thanksgiving for the time and dedication of the Sunday school staff, the choir director and choir members, petitions for a family who had lost a member, an 11-year old who had cancer, and the church secretary's sister who wanted to get pregnant. The chains are also used to help communicate upcoming events like the church picnic or voters meeting.

Another congregation with 11 prayer chains assigns a different segment of the ministry to each chain. One chain prays for the pastor, another the principal, and another the assistant pastor. Some prayer members review the weekly bulletin and pray for the boards, the elders, the Sunday school teachers, and those who are in the hospital. Another focuses on praying for the evangelism callers.

Some group leaders cultivate intercession by making calls to members asking about their needs, "Our prayer chain wants to pray for you. What can we pray for?" *"For My house will be called a house of prayer for all the peoples" (Isaiah 56:7).*

One congregation had prayer teams praying during worship services for the pastor and those in attendance. They especially pray for those in attendance who might not be believers. Leaders at Redeemer have found the best way to promote the prayer chain is through personal invitation. They also put notices in the bulletin each month and include articles on prayer in the monthly newsletter.

Another frequent suggestion was to solicit prayer requests. There are several ways to accomplish this: 1) Have members write prayer requests on slips of paper as they arrive at church and place them at the altar before the worship service begins. During the service the pastor or elders take turns praying for these requests. 2) Have the pastor solicit verbal requests during the service from adults and children. 3) Collect written requests during the service and have prayer teams pray for them during each week. 4) List prayer requests in the bulletin and ask members to pray for the unsaved, inactive, and the sick.

Other suggestions include: 1) Encourage members to become involved in intercessory prayer and establish prayer partners; 2) Begin prayer groups like *Moms in Touch*; 3) Organize prayer breakfasts, retreats, and vigils; 4) Teach members about prayer during sermons and Bible studies; 5) Advertise prayer resources available in your church-school library; 6) Promote seminars, resources, and newsletters about prayer.

Family Shield Ministries has numerous audiocassettes and CDs on the topic of prayer; and Concordia Publishing House has numerous books, products, and resources on prayer. So do other publishers.

Pray now for your pastor and church leaders. Pray for workers for the ripe harvest of souls. Pray for families. Pray Christians will put on the full armor of God, stand firm against the schemes of the evil one, and take up the shield of faith (Ephesians 6:13-16). *"With all prayer and petition pray at all times in the Spirit, and with this in view, be on the alert with all perseverance and petition for all the saints" (Ephesians 6:18).*

Begin at the Beginning

"Do you really believe that God created the world and all that is in it?" Has anyone ever asked you this type of question? How did you respond? Often, the first opportunity to witness will emerge when someone asks a question about God or the Bible.

My answer to the above question would sound something like this, "Yes, I believe God created the world and all that is in it! Isn't it a marvelous creation? Do you believe in God?" I might go on to say, "Did you know the Bible never tries to prove God's existence?" The book of Genesis just begins with the words, "In the beginning God created the heavens and the earth."

> Debate usually doesn't convince anyone to place his or her faith in Christ! Sometimes it pushes them further away.

The creation is a good place to begin witnessing. Too often Christians think they have to prove that evolution is false before they can witness. If you want to debate creation vs. evolution, that's fine, but, make sure you are equipped to do so. I prefer to allow the Word of God, which is in the Sword of the Spirit, and the Holy Spirit, who draws unbelievers to Himself, to do the work. Debate usually doesn't convince anyone to place his or her faith in Christ! Sometimes it pushes them further away. I would strongly suggest you become familiar with books, audiocassettes, and videos by recognized Christians on the topic of creation vs. evolution. Then give or loan these resources to your friend or co-worker.

Become familiar with creation details. Start by investigating and asking what God created on each of the first six days of creation (Genesis 1:3-31) and what He did on the seventh day (Genesis 2:2-3).

Spark interest by asking questions about God's Word. Search your Bible concordance and see how many verses you can find that refer to creation. Ask if they understand what it means when we say the Bible is the inspired Word of God. Other questions that might spark interest include: "After which creation or day did God say, 'It is good or it is not good...'?" "Why do you think He said, 'It is not good...'?" "What do you think it means that we were created in God's image?" "Who named the animals?" "Aside from Genesis, where else is creation referred to in the Bible?" (One answer is Psalm 139:13, *For you created my inmost being" (NIV).* If they give this answer ask them, "What is God talking about in this verse?")

The following is a more difficult question you may or may not want to ask. "In Genesis 1:26, God said, *'Let Us make man in Our image, according to Our likeness; and let them rule over the fish of the sea and over the birds of the sky and over the cattle and over all the earth, and over every creeping thing that creeps on the earth.'* If God is one, who is the 'us' in this passage?"

The Bible states that Christ created the world. In Colossians 1:16 the Bible states, *"For by Him all things were created, both in the heavens and on earth, visible and invisible, whether thrones or dominions or rulers or authorities—all things have been created through Him and for Him. He is before all things, and in Him all things hold together. He is also head of the body, the church; and He is the beginning, the first born from the dead, so that He Himself will come to have first place in everything."* In John 1:1-5 we read, *"In the beginning was the Word, and the Word was with God, and the Word was God. He was in the beginning with God. All things came into being through Him, and apart from Him nothing came into being that has come into being. In Him was life, and the life was the Light of men. The Light shines in the darkness, and the darkness did not comprehend it."* In 1 Corinthians 8:6 we read, *"Yet for us there is but one God, the Father, from whom are all things and we exist for Him; and one Lord, Jesus Christ, by whom are all things, and we exist through Him."* A book to share with those interested in learning more about Christ is *More Than a Carpenter* by Josh McDowell.

"Always (be) ready to make a defense to everyone who asks you to give an account for the hope that is in you, yet with gentleness and reverence" (1 Peter 3:15b).

Obstacles and Barriers in Witnessing

"Sharon left you? I don't know why you're so surprised and upset Eric. I told you to get your life in order and begin going to church, but you never listened to me! Every weekend you were off hunting and drinking with your buddies. Now, maybe you'll listen to my advice!"

The statement above is an example of how some Christians cause barriers when they try to witness. They project an attitude of insensitivity or superiority. They may think they are witnessing, but are actually preaching "the Law" or "good works." When we say, "Go to church and everything will be all right," or "Stop smoking," "Stop drinking," or whatever, we are not sharing the love and forgiveness Christ offers us, and we are not witnessing effectively.

Yes, we need to hear the Law to recognize our sin, but those who do not know Christ also need to know Jesus died for every sin they have committed in the past and sins they may commit in the future. How often we hear, "After I've cleaned up my life I'll consider faith in Christ." When we hear this we should respond, "If you are trying to clean up your life without Christ, you will fail." Tell these people forgiveness and eternal life is ours through faith in Christ. This is Good News everyone needs to hear!

> If you are trying to clean up your life without Christ, you will fail.

Some of you who are reading this may be thinking, "Doesn't the author know we witness by the way we live?" Yes, when we live a life that reflects and glorifies God, unbelievers will be drawn to us. However, we must also be prepared to answer questions such as: "Would you pray for me?" "Tell me about this God you trust so much." "Do you really believe the Bible is God's Word?" When we live our faith we become salt and light in the world, people will see our good works and glorify our Father in heaven. *(See Matthew 5:13-16).*

As we witness, we must remember, no one can come to faith in Christ by seeing our good works. They must hear the saving Gospel message of what Christ has done for them. God's Word says, *"For I am not ashamed of the gospel, for it is the power of God for salvation"* (Romans 1:16a). We have forgiveness and eternal life as a free gift from God because of Christ's sacrifice on the cross for us.

Other barriers include misunderstandings about what it means to be a Christian. Satan has deceived many into believing their good works save them, instead of the death and resurrection of Jesus Christ.

Others think if you believe in God or go to church you are a Christian. Believing in God and going to church do not make someone a Christian. God's Word tells us, *"And there is salvation in no one else; for there is* no other name under heaven that has been given among men, by which we must be saved" *(Acts 4:12)*. A Christian is someone who has salvation (sometimes referred to as eternal life or being born again) because of their faith in Christ.

Now, what about objections raised when you are trying to share the Gospel message with unbelievers? Some of the objections you may hear:

- I don't believe in God.
- I don't believe the Bible is inspired by God or relevant to my life.
- Church bores me. I don't get anything out of it, so why should I bother to attend?
- All religions are the same. What difference does it make which church I attend?

Remember, we can't argue people into heaven or convince them to believe or have faith. We might win the argument, but lose the soul. It is God's Word, the Gospel, and the Holy Spirit that convert individuals; we don't. Some people raise objections because they want to get you off a subject that is making them uncomfortable; but at other times objections are raised because the person truly wants an answer. Rely upon the Holy Spirit to guide and direct you as you witness. Recall Colossians 4:5-6 *"Conduct yourselves with wisdom toward outsiders, making the most of the opportunity. Let your speech always be with grace, as though seasoned with salt, so that you will know how you should respond to each person."*

Some issues must be accepted by faith. We will not always have an answer, nor should we always try to answer all questions individuals raise as we share the Gospel. Sometimes, we must just speak the Gospel and God's Word.

Some objections can be addressed. One objection some may find hard to address is when someone says, "I don't believe the Bible is inspired by God." Certainly one approach is to just use the Word of God anyway, but what else might we share when someone raises this objection? Consider sharing the following:

1. *Prophecies and Their Fulfillment in Christ.* Most people do not understand the importance of prophecies. Explain that prophecies

are predictions by prophets of God recorded in the Old Testament and fulfilled in the New Testament. The prophets shared details concerning Christ's life that was written hundreds and sometimes thousands of years before His birth.

Quote two or three of these prophecies from memory, or look several up together. A few samples are listed below:

- A virgin will bear a son and we will call Him Emmanuel (Isaiah 7:14/Matthew 1:18, 23).
- Out of Egypt (Hosea 11:1/Matthew 2:14-15).
- Despised and rejected by men (Isaiah 53:3/John 1:11).
- The King comes riding a donkey (Zechariah 9:9/John 12:13-15).
- A close friend will betray Him (Psalm 41:9/Mark 14:10)
- Sold for 30 pieces of silver (Zechariah 11:12/Matthew 26:15).
- Did not open His mouth (Isaiah 53:7/Matthew 26:62-63).

2. *Why Does the Bible Continue to Survive?* The Bible has been the most maligned and hated book in history, yet it continues to survive. It is also the number one best selling book in the world. God is behind its survival!

3. *The Bible Has Amazing Unity.* It includes 66 books written over 1500 years by 39 men from various walks of life. Yet all the pieces fit perfectly. God is behind its unity.

4. *The Bible Has Power to Change Lives.* Tell them about Christ and what He has done for you. Tell them about others whose lives have been changed forever as they read the Bible. Explain that God can change their lives too. Encourage them to read it and see for themselves.

Barriers, obstacles, and objections will continue to arise as we witness for Christ. When they do, recall 1 Peter 3:15, *"Always be prepared to give an answer to everyone who asks you to give the reason for the hope that you have. But do this with gentleness and respect..." (NIV).* May God grant us His wisdom as we live our faith and learn to witness for Him!

Part 2

Witnessing Begins At Home

"These words, which I am commanding you today, shall be on your heart. You shall teach them diligently to your children and shall talk of them when you sit in your house and when you walk by the way and when you lie down and when you rise up" *(Deuteronomy 6:6-7).*

Growing Strong Christian Families

Raising children in today's world is a joy, a privilege, and a challenge! Parenting is perhaps the most important job you will ever have. When you became a parent, God gave you a most precious gift—a child of His to care for as His representative here on earth.

Over the past 50 years there have been dramatic changes in families and our culture. Up through the 1960s there was a Judeo-Christian heritage that guided families. Today we are moving toward godlessness or at least spiritualism without Christ. Up through the 1960s there was Biblical awareness. Today individuals, within and outside of the Church, are often Biblically ignorant. Up through the 1960s there was friendship with neighbors. Today we are isolated from neighbors, and many families are fractured. Up through the 1960s schools, media, and government seemed to support religion. Today it often seems they oppose religion or at least Christianity.

Today only 27 percent of American households fit the traditional model of decades past. In 1960, 60 percent of families had a mother who stayed at home and a dad who worked. Today this represents seven percent of the population. Today one of three households consists of a single parent with one or more children. Sixty percent of children under 16 will experience the divorce of their parents. Children are having children; 1.3 million children live with teenage parents, only half of whom are married. Between 1971 and 1989, the number of teens in psychiatric hospitals rose from 6,500 to 200,000, and the suicide rate of children and adolescents has tripled.

A recent Gallop Poll demonstrates some of the challenges facing Christians in equipping children, parents, and families to know, grow, and go for Christ. It shows that:

- Households headed by unmarried partners (most involving people living together out of wedlock) grew by almost 72 percent during the past decade.
- Households headed by single mothers or fathers increased by 25 and 62 percent respectively.
- For the first time the nuclear family dropped below 25 percent of households.
- Of all babies born, 33 percent were to unmarried women, compared to only 3.8 percent in 1940.
- Cohabitation increased by close to 1,000 percent from 1960 to 1998, and the households headed by same-sex couples are soaring.
- Children raised by their mothers alone are 30 percent more likely to use drugs than those living in supportive two-parent homes according to a study by Joseph Califano, Jr., president of the National Center on Addiction and Substance Abuse at Columbia University. The study notes that, "A child living in a two-parent family whose relationship with the father is poor, is 68 percent more likely to smoke, drink, and use drugs than teens living in an average two-parent household." Teens with the lowest risk of substance abuse are those who have two parents who eat meals with their children, take them to religious services, help them with homework, attend their games and activities, mentor their conduct, give them praise and discipline, and cultivate a loving family relationship.

We must shield our children and families from false teachings of the culture and dangerous beliefs, reach out with the Gospel to those who do not know Christ, and equip Christians to serve and witness. We must help individuals recognize the spiritual battle they are in and encourage them to use the shield of faith. *"Put on the full armor of God, so that you will be able to stand firm against the schemes of the devil. ...taking up the shield of faith with which you will be able to extinguish all the flaming arrows of the evil one. And take the helmet of salvation, and the sword of the Spirit, which is the word of God"* (Ephesians 6:11, 16-17).

Building strong families takes prayer, an abundance of forgiveness, and reliance upon the Lord. It's a difficult task to raise children and grow healthy families in today's world. Did you know that 25 years of research has shown six major qualities of strong families? This information is taken from *Fantastic Families* by Dr. Nick and Nancy Stinnett and Joe Beam. The six traits include:

1. *Commitment* (Genesis 2:23-24). Members of strong families are dedicated to promoting each other's welfare and happiness. They value the unity of the family.
2. *Appreciation and Affection* (Genesis 2:23-24; Psalm 127:3-4). Members of strong families show appreciation for each other a great deal. They can feel how good a family is.
3. *Positive Communication* (Ephesians 6:1-4). Members of strong families have good communication skills and spend large amounts of time talking with each other.
4. *Time Together* (Deuteronomy 6:7; Proverbs 22:6). Strong families spend time—quality time—with each other.
5. *Spiritual Well-being* (Deuteronomy 11:18-21; Acts 2:38-39; Ephesians 6:4). Strong families have a sense of a greater good or power of God in their life. That belief gives them strength and purpose.
6. *The Ability to Cope with Stress and Crises* (Ephesians 6:4; 1 Thessalonians 2:11). Members of strong families are able to view stress or crises as opportunities to grow.

Remember that strong families are not without problems. Strong families have many difficulties. Their loved ones become seriously ill, there is unemployment, death of a loved one, car accidents, disasters, and every other problem known to humankind. But strong families press on in the midst of their challenges. Parents and grandparents model their faith and persevere. And they grow in the process!

You and your congregation can equip individuals and families for the spiritual battle and learn to rely upon God's power, the Gospel, the forgiveness of Christ, the Word of God, His weapons, and prayer. *"Do not be terrified; do not be discouraged, for the Lord your God will be with you wherever you go" (Joshua 1:9b, NIV). "Thanks be to God! He gives us the victory through our Lord Jesus Christ" (1 Corinthians 15:57, NIV). "We have this treasure in jars of clay to show that this all-surpassing power is from God and not from us. We are hard pressed on every side, but not crushed; perplexed, but not in despair; persecuted, but not abandoned; struck down, but not destroyed" (2 Corinthians 4:7-9, NIV).*

Fun Family Devotions

It's tough, isn't it? Even in Christian families tempers sometimes flare. Christians sometimes find themselves irritated by insignificant events.

Then, too, we don't talk with one another about our faith or about our Savior as often as we might like. Family devotions scare many Christians. We all know we should worship and pray together as a family, but sometimes we don't because we just don't know how!

The following "Fun Family Devotions" can be done at home. They will help you share your faith with your children and grandchildren. As you begin, you may want to try to spend time together once each week rather than every night. Plan to use one of the ideas in your weekly family fun night each week.

BIBLE TICK-TACK-TOE

If you know how to play regular tick-tack-toe, you will enjoy this adapted version. Use it to review Bible stories, Bible characters, books of the Bible, or places in Scripture.

To begin, draw a large tick-tack-toe grid on a piece of paper. Inside each square of the grid write the name of a Bible character or a question about God's Word.

Then split the family into two teams. The first team chooses a character from the grid and tells something about that person. If the team chooses a square with "Moses," they might say, "Moses led God's people through the desert."

If the team makes a correct statement, they may place their mark (an X or O) over "Moses" on the grid. If the statement is incorrect, the other team may challenge them. Then they may not mark the grid.

Take turns, and as in regular tick-tack-toe, the team with the three Xs or three Os in a row wins.

To begin a new game, make a new grid with new names, places, Bible books, or Bible stories.

You can adapt this game for younger children by placing pictures in the grid instead of words. Cut these from the Sunday school leaflets your children bring home. For example, use a cross, a Bible, a picture of Jesus, or a dove.

As a closing prayer, use something like this: Heavenly Father, we praise You for loving us even when we were sinners. Thank You for sending Jesus to die for us. Thank You for giving us each other in this family. Help us to love You and one another better each day. In Jesus' name. Amen."

BIBLE CHARADES

In this version of an old favorite, Mom or Dad chooses a familiar Bible story for one or more of the children to act out. The others in the group try to guess the story.

You may want to prepare by looking through the Bible for ideas. Write these on small slips of paper. Then let older children pick a slip. Talk about the stories as you do them. Remember to stress God's love and patient forgiveness for His people despite their frequent faithlessness.

Here are some stories you may wish to include:

Noah and the Ark (Genesis 6:15-22); Moses Brings the Ten Commandments Down from Sinai (Exodus 20:1-18); Joseph and the Coat of Many Colors (Genesis 37:3); Jonah Runs Away from God's Call (Jonah 1:1-3); Jesus Feeds 5,000 (Matthew 14:15-21); Jesus' Arrest (John 18:3-13), Jesus' Death and Burial (John 19); or Jesus Appears to Thomas (John 20:24-29).

Of course, once you begin you and your children will think of many other examples. If you have a larger or extended family gathering, you might even divide into teams and award points for correct answers.

Conclude the evening with family prayer time. Make up your prayers together. You may want to write one down and read it when you have finished it. Remember to thank God for His unending love and forgiveness in Jesus. Also remember to thank Him for your family and for the good times you have had together.

BIBLE MEMORY FUN

God has promised many blessings to those who treasure His Word in their hearts. Yet, many children find it hard to memorize Scripture verses. Many adults have not taken the time or effort to learn a new verse since their own childhood. Why not try learning one new verse a week—as a family? Playing games may be the key.

> Continue taking away the cards and saying the verse until you have removed the whole verse from the table and you can recite the verse from memory.

Choose a verse, write it and the reference on a large piece of paper, and then cut it apart—word by word or phrase by phrase. Hide these word cards around the house before devotion time. (Make sure you have at least one word for each family member.)

Tell the family how many word cards you have hidden, and then give them the "Go" signal. At this point, everyone searches the house for the word cards. When all the word cards have been found, everyone should hurry back to the living room or kitchen to assemble the Bible verse. Find the verse in the Bible to check your answer.

Talk together about what the verse means and how it might apply to specific problems or situations your family faces right now. Read the words together several times. Then let the youngest family member take away one of the word cards. Read the verse again, adding the missing word. Continue taking away the cards and saying the verse until you have removed the whole verse from the table and you can recite the verse from memory.

Save your word cards for review next time you play "Bible Memory Fun." End the evening by praying together. You might sit or stand in a circle and hold hands. Then take turns around the circle thanking God for something about your family. If it seems awkward at first, keep trying. After some practice you will begin to feel more comfortable.

M&Ms REMIND ME OF GOD

"Mom, wake up! It's time for us to get ready to go to church."

"Dad, can I invite Larry to go to church and Sunday school with us this weekend?"

"Wally, would you like to come to Sunday school with me this Sunday?"

"Steven, let's play church. I'll be the pastor."

"Coreen, M&Ms remind me of God. Want to tell me how?"

Sometimes our children witness to us. At other times, we share our faith with them. What's happening in your family? Are you helping your children to share their faith with others? If not, why not begin today?

The following is a children's message you can share with your children or grandchildren during your family devotions or with your Sunday school class. Before you begin, have ready one large bag of M&Ms and enough small individual sandwich bags to give two bags to each child.

Begin by asking, "How many of you like M&Ms?"

"Good! Then you'll like this devotion. 'M&Ms remind me of God.' See the two large Ms on the bag? The first 'M' reminds me of the Messiah. Jesus is our Messiah. He came to earth to live the life we are unable to live. He died on the cross for our sins and rose again to assure us our eternal life. When I know Jesus as my Messiah, God gives me many opportunities to do ministry or works of service for Him. The second 'M' reminds me of ministry—sharing the Good News in my words and actions."

"There are a lot more ways that M&Ms remind me of God. I'll need your help now." Hold up a green M&M and ask, "How does green remind you of God?"

Allow children to respond by raising their hands. Their answers might include "new life," "green leaves," "new birth," "grass," and "the world God created for me."

"What about yellow?" I've used this devotion several times, and at least one of the children always says, "the sun."

"That's right. When I think of the sun, I think of how it gives us life. I also think of the Son of God. He, too, gives us life—life in heaven with Him forever."

"What about brown?" This may be a little harder for the children. If they can't think of anything, give them a hint. One second grader responded, "The brown reminds me of the wood that the cross was made from that Jesus died on." Another answer might be "God made everybody special and unique. He made each of us different. Some of us are brown in color, and some of us are lighter."

Children might also respond with answers such as "the earth," "trunks of trees," and even "candy." Praise their answers! Let them be creative!

The blue M&Ms will bring thoughts like "the ocean," "water," and "blueberry muffins."

Ask, "How does red remind us of God?" Children who have attended Sunday school regularly will usually think of the blood of Christ. I elaborate a little on this one. "Yes, and remember that the blood of Christ washes away our sins, the bad things we do each day."

Another answer often given for red is "God's love," represented by hearts.

Then you might ask, "How does the shape of an M&M remind you of God?" Allow time for the children to think and respond. Affirm their answers. Explain that, "The circle reminds me that God is never ending. He has no beginning and no end."

"What about the taste of M&Ms?" Explain that God gives us food and supplies our daily needs. He gives us candy that tastes good!

As I close the devotion, I tell the children I am going to give them two bags with various colors of M&Ms inside. (I put at least one of each color into small plastic bags, but you can purchase individual bags of M&Ms as well.)

I tell them, after they check with mom and dad, that they may eat the M&Ms in one of the bags. Then I tell them, "I'd like you to use the other bag to tell a friend how M&Ms remind you of God. Will you please do that? When you do, you will be witnessing to your faith in Jesus, sharing the Good News with someone."

Close by praying: "Thank You, Jesus, for being our Messiah and for forgiving us when we sin. Thank You for loving us. Help us share Your love with others. In Your name we pray. Amen."

Witnessing—A Family Affair

"Suzie, it's time to pray. Look at mommy; fold your hands like this."

"Bobby, look at that sunset. Didn't God create a beautiful world for us to live in?"

"Jimmie, why don't we pray together about your argument with Sarah?"

> God's plan is for families to tell the next generation about the praiseworthy deeds of the Lord.

"Sharon! Joseph! Are you ready? It's time to leave for church and Sunday school!"

How did you come to know Jesus as your Savior and Lord? Did you grow up in a Christian home where your parents shared and modeled their faith? Or, did you come to faith because a sister, brother, stepparent, grandparent, aunt, uncle, or cousin loved you enough to tell you about the Lord and His wonderful work for you and the cross of Calvary?

Witnessing is a family affair. God's plan is for families to tell the next generation about the praiseworthy deeds of the Lord. *"These words, which I am commanding you today, shall be on your heart. You shall teach them diligently to your sons* [and daughters] *and shall talk of them when you sit in your house and when you walk by the way and when you lie down and when you rise up" (Deuteronomy 6:6-7).*

God tells us not to conceal His great and mighty acts from our children, but to tell the next generation the praises of the Lord, His strength, and the wondrous works that He has done.

Sadly, Satan's attack on the family has caused many families to abandon belief in God completely. Millions of parents never speak of God or Jesus Christ. The only time these children hear Jesus' name is when it is used as a curse word. Their view of a Christian is obtained by watching television programs. And how many of us have seen a good portrayal of a Christian recently on television?

We need to ask the Lord for guidance in raising our children to rely upon God, know and love Jesus Christ as their Savior and Lord, and to walk daily with Him. What a wonderful mission opportunity to witness within our homes to our children! As we raise our children to know and love the Lord we must become aware of Satan's schemes and learn to use the Shield of Faith against his fiery missiles.

We are in a spiritual battle (Ephesians 6:12). Satan is the enemy. His ultimate aim is to keep you and your family members from ever knowing Christ as Savior and Lord and/or to corrupt or destroy your faith in Him.

Families need help in fighting off Satan's schemes and the negative influences of the secular world. How do we, as Christians, put on the full armor of God so we can stand firm against Satan's schemes? Read Ephesians 6:10-18. It addresses spiritual warfare. It begins, "*Finally, be strong in the Lord and in the strength of His might. Put on the full armor of God, so that you will be able to stand firm against the schemes of the devil.*"

> Satan uses subtle means to get us to put family, job, material items, sports, or power before the Lord.

Satan has convinced many to believe non-biblical truths. He deceives people into believing that they are saved by their good works instead of through Christ's death and resurrection. This is why the New Age movement, cults, the occult, and so many false religions continue to arise and increase; and why nearly half of all Christians think Satan is just a symbol of evil and not a living being. (Source: *What American's Believe* by George Barna, p. 205.)

Satan uses subtle means to get us to put family, job, material items, sports, or power before the Lord. It's when we say, "I don't have time for Bible study," or "Missing church this week is all right because we are going on a family outing," that Satan's subtle schemes are working in our lives.

Satan wants us to doubt our faith. He likes us to think we're not good enough or don't know enough to witness for the Lord.

Satan continues to place temptations of the flesh, materialism, the media's negative influence, and family problems in our path. He tempts us to turn away from God and toward the "things" of this world.

But Ephesians 6:10-11 tells us we can resist Satan's schemes. How? By putting on the full armor of God and using the weapons He supplies in facing daily situations. We are to:

1. Keep our eyes on Jesus, the author and preserver of our faith (Hebrews 12:2).
2. Remember Jesus died for our sins, and rose from the dead (1 Corinthians 15:1-8).
3. Recall Christ's promise to be with us always (Matthew 28:20).

4. Stay in the Word. It is the Sword of the Spirit (Ephesians 6:17). *"For the Word of God is living and active and sharper than any two-edged sword, and piercing as far as the division of soul and spirit" (Hebrews 4:12). "All Scripture is inspired by God and profitable for teaching, for reproof, for correction, for training in righteousness; so that the man [or woman] of God may be adequate, equipped for every good work" (2 Timothy 3:16-17).*

5. Worship regularly (Hebrews 10:25).

6. Enter into fellowship with other believers (1 John 1:7).

7. Pray. *"Pray for one another and build one another up" (1 Thessalonians 5:11). "Ask and it will be given to you; seek, and you will find; knock, and it will be opened to you" (Matthew 7:7). "Again I say to you, that if two of you agree on earth about anything that they may ask, it shall be done for them by My Father who is in heaven. For where two or three have gathered together in My name, I am there in their midst" (Matthew 18:19-20).*

8. Remember Satan is the defeated foe and Jesus is the victorious reigning King. With God's power and the help of the Holy Spirit who lives in us we can resist Satan's attacks (2 Timothy 4:18).

9. Use God's power—the Gospel of Jesus Christ.

Read 1 Corinthians 15:1-8. This is the Gospel – Christ died for our sins. When Satan makes you think you cannot witness, recall God's promise to give you the words to speak in the hour you need them. *"But when they hand you over, do not worry about how or what you are to say; for it will be given you in that hour what you are to say. For it is not you who speak, but it is the Spirit of your Father who speaks in you" (Matthew 10:19-20).*

God is our shield (Psalm 28:7) and He gives us the Shield of Faith against the flaming missiles Satan fires at us daily (Ephesians 6:16). Use the Shield of Faith!

Witnessing should be a family affair! Are you sharing your faith with your children and grandchildren? Have Satan's schemes been active and alive in your family? If so, begin using the Shield of Faith to resist Satan's attacks. Pray. Communicate effectively. Love. Laugh. Then take time to tell your children what Jesus means to you and what He's done for them. You'll be glad you did!

Witnessing Begins at Home

Often, when I present programs at congregations and schools, a mom or dad will come up afterwards and say, "I wish God would give me a mission in life."

I respond, "God has given you a mission. Your mission, and my mission, is to raise our children to know and love Jesus Christ. It isn't an easy job—in fact, raising Christian children in today's world is probably the most difficult job you will ever experience. It doesn't happen by osmosis. It takes prayer, time, energy, concern and care. It takes a lot of modeling of the faith, as well as speaking of the Lord and His love, as we walk and talk with our children.

Children are a precious gift from the Lord (Psalm 127:3). He has given us the responsibility and privilege of raising our children so they grow up physically, emotionally, and spiritually. Yes, witnessing begins in the home.

You may have begun sharing your faith with your children while they were too young to even remember. You took them to be baptized as infants, taught them to fold their hands and pray at mealtime and bedtime, prayed with and for them, and took them to church and Sunday school.

You continued to share your faith as they grew up into Him (Ephesians 4:15). You helped them memorize Bible verses and complete lessons for Sunday school, Bible classes, and confirmation. You told them how much you loved them, how proud you were of them, spent time with them, and talked about the Lord and what it means to have faith in Christ in everyday activities as you drove them to dance lessons, scouts, gym classes, school and church, ate meals and washed dishes together.

> One aspect of living out our faith within the home means recognizing and admitting our failures and sinfulness.

One of the best ways to help your child know and love the Lord is to talk not only about what we should and should not do (the Law,) but to model and live our faith within the home.

One aspect of living out our faith within the home means recognizing and admitting our failures and sinfulness. As Christians we are saints and sinners. We are in need of daily forgiveness from the Lord. We also need forgiveness from those within our families. 1 John 1:9 says, *"If we confess our sins, He is faithful and righteous to forgive us our sins and to cleanse us from all unrighteousness."* God forgives us for Jesus' sake. So will a loving, Christ-centered family.

The most difficult place to live our faith is in the home. James 5:16 says, *"Therefore, confess your sins to one another, and pray for one another."* Are you confessing your sins and praying for each other regularly? If not, why not begin today?

Doesn't it seem like anger or bitterness erupts easier with loved ones than with anyone else? Both parents and children say and do things that cause arguments and problems. In Ephesians 4:31-32 we are told, *"Let all bitterness and wrath and anger and clamor and slander be put away from you, along with all malice. Be kind to one another, tender-hearted, forgiving each other, just as God in Christ also has forgiven you."* What a wonderful Bible verse to use within our homes. Why not post it on the refrigerator as a constant reminder for you and your family?

Little things can also demonstrate our faith and witness to family members within the home. Hanging pictures of Jesus or Bible passages, wearing a lapel pin that reminds us of our Savior and Lord, having family devotions together, praying together at mealtime and bedtime, listening to Christian radio within the home, taking children to a Christian bookstore and letting them purchase a tape or book, or talking about the Lord as we drive our children to sports and school activities.

Consider how you have shared God's love with your children this week. If you're having trouble finding time, begin watching for quiet times to share your faith.

As you share your faith with your children, many opportunities to share with other relatives, friends, and neighbors will also occur. The following are just a few examples:

- Our daughter had invited a neighborhood friend, whose parents were unchurched, on a camping trip. We played Bible Charades and discussed the Bible verses. This game opened up several conversations about Jesus with our neighbor—an opportunity to witness.
- I was baby-sitting for a friend's eight-year-old daughter one summer. The children and I read several Bible stories together. My children wanted to get on to other activities, but Jill was so excited to learn stories from the Bible. "Do we have to stop? Please teach me more!"

    When her mother came to pick her up she said, "Mom, the Meyers read stories from the Bible. Why don't we begin doing that,

Mom? It was fun!" Although Jill's parents attended church, they had never used the Bible within the home—another non-threatening opportunity to witness.

- Suzie attended Sunday school, vacation Bible school, and church with my daughter, Coreen. Her parents were not Christians. During a thunderstorm Suzie was afraid and prayed out loud to Jesus. "Jesus, please keep us safe. I'm scared. Be with me and Mom." Her mother responded, "Oh, no, Suzie, you can't pray to Jesus. He isn't God." Suzie answered, "Yes, He is, Mom. We learned that Jesus is both God and man at school. We *can* pray to Jesus!"

  Her mother asked me the next day, "Do you really teach that you can pray to Jesus?" Suzie's mother had misunderstood what Christians believe about Christ. Her daughter taught her that not only can we pray, but that we can pray to Jesus. Out of the mouths of babes—children witnessing to parents!

- The Mitchells' eight-year-old son invited a new friend who had recently moved into the neighborhood to have dinner with them. During dinner this family learned the boy, his brother, and mother did not attend Sunday school or church. They extended an invitation for them to visit their congregation. Some months later the entire family committed their life to Christ, were baptized, and became active members of a Christian congregation.

  The Mitchells didn't know it, but this young eight-year old boy they had befriended would become a minister one day. He would lead hundreds to the foot of the cross.

Witnessing begins at home. It really isn't so difficult, is it? All this family did was share a meal and their faith in Christ with a young boy. They showed interest in his life by asking questions about his family. When they discovered they didn't attend church, they invited them to visit their congregation. But God was behind the invitation! Remember God's Word says, *"I planted, Apollos watered, but God was causing the growth" (1 Corinthians 3:6).*

Remember, as you model and share your faith within the home, God will open doors to reach beyond your immediate family to others. Why not begin with prayer? Why not begin at home? Why not begin today?

A Mother Who Shared Her Faith

My mom was in the hospital. It was serious, but as usual, she wasn't thinking about herself. She was thinking about her family. "Kay, did I tell you that Diane Winterer works at this hospital? Dad and I saw her in the emergency room the day I was admitted. You haven't seen each other in years. Why don't you go downstairs right now and see if you can talk to her." I did go downstairs and found my old childhood friend. Diane and I had a quick, but enjoyable reunion.

My mother, Eunice Schoenberger, passed from death to everlasting life (John 5:24) on May 5, 1998. She was a mother who shared her faith with her husband, my sisters, me, eight grandchildren, one great grandson, and hundreds of family members and friends. She lived 77 years before entering into the heavenly Kingdom.

God's Word exhorts parents and grandparents to share their faith with the next generation. *"Listen, O my people, to my in-struction; Incline your ears to the words of my mouth. …We will not conceal them from their children, but tell to the generation to come the praises of the Lord, and His strength and the wondrous works that He has done. For He established a testimony in Jacob, and appointed a law in Israel, which He commanded our fathers, that they should teach them to their children, that the generation to come might know, even the children yet to be born, That they may arise and tell them to their children, that they should put their confidence in God" (Psalm 78:1,4-7).*

My prayer is that you will be encouraged to share your faith! As I thought about my mother, several key phrases stood out about her life. I want to share them with you.

1. *Mom was always there for all of us.* She was available and involved in her family's lives. She never worked outside the home, but she was always actively involved with family, friends, and in the community.

2. *She showed her love through words and actions.* When we were young she was our Brownie and Girl Scout leader, a room mother, and Sunday school teacher. Her involvement and love didn't

change as we grew up and began having families of our own.

3. *Family was always a top priority.* She was an involved wife, mother and grandmother. Until a few years before she died, Mom would have the entire family over for dinner at least twice a month! Yes, I said twice a month! These family gatherings would include three daughters, their husbands, eight grandchildren, and more recently granddaughters' husbands and children.

4. *She used her spiritual gifts in service to others.* Her spiritual gifts included service, hospitality, and administration. She was extremely organized and chaired many committees and projects over the years.

5. *She knew Christ as her Savior and talked about her relationship with Him regularly.* Mom wasn't perfect, but she knew she was forgiven! She didn't just share her faith with her family, but with others as well. She taught Sunday school for years, she was an active prayer chain member, attended Bible studies, and offered to help neighbors and friends.

6. *She was confident of her eternal life.* Mom was only ill for seven short weeks. Following her surgery she said, "Kay, I'll fight to live for my family. But, I want you to know I'm not afraid to die. I know where I'm going when I die and I'm not afraid. Heaven is a much better place!"

7. *She was involved in the community.* Mom was not only active in the lives of her family; she was also active in the community. She and my father, Joseph Schoenberger, were active in many community organizations.

I praise and thank God for my mother! I'm thankful she was always there for me. I am most thankful for her love. And most of all, I'm thankful that she shared her faith with me. This is God's plan! He wants us to share God's Word and our faith with our families. Don't wait! Share your faith today!

"These words, which I am commanding you today, shall be on your heart. You shall teach them diligently to your sons [and daughters] and shall talk of them when you sit in your house and when you walk by the

way and when you lie down and when you rise up. You shall bind them as a sign on your hand and they shall be as frontals on your forehead. You shall write them on the doorposts of your house and on your gates" (Deuteronomy 6:6-9).

Parents—Teach Your Children to Pray and Share Their Faith

"Mom, today the new neighbor, Tyler, said he doesn't attend Sunday school or church. I invited him to come with us this week. Can we pick him up?"

* * *

"My daughter, Lisa, and the next door neighbor's little girl are close friends and play together all the time. Yesterday I overheard them talking. Lisa was telling Christy that Jesus loved her. Christy's dad's is an alcoholic. Her mother never attends church. It was so exciting to hear my daughter sharing her faith with her friend!"

* * *

"Teresa, we're having a Bible study after school. Would you like to join us?"

* * *

"These words, which I am commanding you today, shall be on your heart. You shall teach them diligently to your sons and shall talk of them when you sit in your house and when you walk by the way and when you lie down and when you rise up" (Deuteronomy 6:6-7). God's Word instructs parents to tell their children about the Lord. We also need to help them learn to share their faith! Children and youth have many opportunities to share their faith at school, sports activities, scouting activities, and as they interact with children and youth in the community.

When do you begin? Begin when they are small. Take them to be baptized or dedicate them to the Lord. Take them to church and Sunday school. Sing Christian songs and play Christian music in the home. Read age-appropriate Christian books and children's Bible stories to them. Allow them to watch Christian videos and DVDs. And talk about the Lord as you walk, travel, and talk about your day's activities.

Recognize that the home is the most difficult place to live the faith. *"Confess your sins to each other and pray for each other so that they may be healed" (James 5:16). "Get rid of all bitterness, rage and anger, brawling and slander along with every kind of malice. Be kind and compassionate to one another, forgiving each other, just as God in Christ forgave you"* (Ephesians 4:31-32, NIV).

Children need to see parents modeling the faith. Living out our Christian faith in the home is not easy. When we fail, which we will, learn to say, "I'm sorry. Will you forgive me?" They will! Children need to see their parent forgive them when they sin, just as Christ has forgiven us. We need to help our children confess their sins to God and help them understand that God forgives them because of Christ (John 3:16).

Children also need to see us pray. Pray for those who are struggling with illness and problems. Pray for those who do not know Christ. Allow your child to see you reading the Bible, having private and family devotions, and living your faith in the home and the community.

A, B, C, one, two, three, thank You, God, for feeding me! Amen.

Prayer is an important part of our faith and is where we begin as we teach our children to share their faith. How do we teach our children to pray and rely upon God for all things? Begin when they are small. Encourage them to fold their hands even before they can talk. Soon they will be saying "Amen" at the end of each prayer. Teach them simple prayers and teach them God's Word. Use prayers that are age-appropriate. My grandson, Seth, and granddaughter, Lizzy, enjoy reciting this simple mealtime prayer, "A, B, C, one, two, three, thank You, God, for feeding me! Amen."

Pray together at mealtime and bedtime. Invite your children to pray for those they know. Encourage them to invite friends to Sunday school and church. Pray for their friends and those who do not know Christ.

Invite different members of the family to lead prayers. Our grandson, Seth, loves to lead the mealtime prayers. One of his favorites is a song sung to the tune of Johnnie Appleseed. "Oh, the Lord is good to me, and so I thank the Lord, for giving me the things I need, the sun, the rain, and the apple trees, the Lord is good to me. Amen."

Once when my husband and I visited our daughter and son-in-law they had a prayer cube on the dining room table. It was made of construction paper. Scotch tape was used to hold it together. The children colored it before my daughter wrote different prayers on each side of the cube. One side said, "Make up a mealtime prayer." Another side had the common table prayer: "Come, Lord Jesus, be our Guest, and let this food to us be blessed. Amen." A child tosses the cube to see which prayer will be recited either by the family together, or by the prayer leader.

Another prayer activity that helps children learn to pray is to make a prayer chain. Small strips of paper are cut and distributed. The paper should be about 2½ inches by 8 inches. Each person is asked to write a prayer on the paper. Adults can help the children write their prayer. After they are written each person shares what he or she has written. Then the slips of paper are stapled into circles, one inside the other. And these prayer chains are put up in the kitchen or dining room. When company comes over you can ask if they have a specific prayer request that they would like to add to your prayer chain. Soon, as you continue to add prayers to the chain, your home is wrapped in prayer!

At bedtime or anytime, talk to your children about their day. Ask them to tell you what was the best thing that happened that day and what was the worst thing that happened. They might tell you about an argument with a friend. After you've discussed these things, include them in your prayers. So in the argument with the friend, you might include in your prayers, "Lord, help Mickey forgive Jimmy and help them become friends again. Amen."

"And that from childhood you have known the sacred writings which are able to give you the wisdom that leads to salvation through faith which is in Christ Jesus" (2 Timothy 3:15).

Fathers—Share Your Life and Faith

My son-in-law, David, takes his responsibility to share his faith and life with his young children very seriously. This fact is evident whenever we attend church with our daughter, son-in-law, and their children. A few Easters ago my husband and I attended the Good Friday service with David and our grandson who was four years old. It was late and we weren't sure Seth would stay awake for the entire service, but he did. As the Good Friday evening service progressed, his father quietly leaned over to explain what was happening and why. Seth took it all in quietly. He had little to say that evening, but as the extended family arrived at his home on Easter he asked, "Papa, is Jesus God?" "Yes." David said. "What a great question, Seth!"

Did you know that fathers are probably the most influential people in children's lives in terms of influencing their faith? Statistics indicate that 43 percent of young adults say they are active in the church today because they had a father who modeled the faith. Five percent are active in church today because they talked about their faith with their fathers. Fathers need to model their faith and talk about faith issues with their children.

A father's influence on his children's faith and life is critical. A father's relationship with his son or daughter is one of the most important factors in whether the child stays close to the Lord throughout his or her life.

How is your relationship with your children? Do you spend time together? Eat meals together? Talk during these meals about the day's events? Do you ask your children questions about their day and listen attentively when they have something to share? Do you attend church together? Do you share your life *and* faith?

Ephesians 6:4 states, *"Fathers, do not provoke your children to anger, but bring them up in the discipline and instruction of the Lord."* Have you ever provoked your children to anger? Maybe by nagging them? Or by losing control of your temper? Or by not listening? Learn to say, "I'm sorry, will you forgive me?"

Maybe you are a father who has never talked to your children about faith issues. How do you begin? Begin now! Teach them to pray at mealtime and bedtime. Read them Bible storybooks appropriate to their age. Sing Christian songs together in the car. Take them to church and Sunday school. Talk to them as you take walks. "Michael, look at that tree and its beautiful leaves. Didn't God make a beautiful world for us to enjoy?" "Annie, sit on my lap. Which story from the children's Bible would you like me to read tonight?" "Andy, how was your Sunday school class today? Can you tell me what the lesson was about?"

As your children mature, encourage them to have private devotional time with the Lord and to read the Bible on their own. Give them a devotional book to read. Go biking, fishing or take long walks with them, or engage in other types of one-on-one activities. As you do these things, talk about God's grace and forgiveness that is theirs through Christ.

What can we learn about fatherhood from God's Word? We learn that the Lord uses imperfect people to accomplish His work, and that many well-know Bible characters made mistakes as fathers! Let's look at a few of them and evaluate what they did right and what they did wrong as fathers.

King David wasn't perfect. He committed adultery with another man's wife. When he learned she was pregnant with his child, he sent her husband into a battle hoping he would be killed (2 Samuel 11). His sins caused him much grief and sorrow.

Did you know David had six wives and many children? Although David loved his children, the Bible indicates that he did not discipline them. A Godly father certainly loves his children, but also disciplines them. Let's review what happened with some of David's children and how his lack of discipline caused serious problems.

One of David's sons, Amnon, raped his half sister Tamar. David was furious, but did nothing (2 Samuel 13:21). David's son Absalom, Tamar's natural brother, murdered Amnon (2 Samuel 13:23-29, 32-33). David still did nothing. Later Absalom conspired against David and usurped the Kingdom (2 Samuel 15 and 18:1-17). When Absalom died, David grieved publicly (2 Samuel 15 and 18:33).

Maybe you've been like David. You love your children but you don't discipline them. Ask the Lord to help you become a better father. And remember that discipline is not punishment. Discipline should be constructive and based on love.

Discipline is training a child in mind and character to enable him or her to become a self-controlled, constructive member of society. This involves training through every type of communication. It includes guidance by example, modeling, verbal instruction, written requests, teaching, and providing learning and fun experiences. Punishment is only one of many ways of discipline and is the most negative format. Guidance toward right thought and action is far superior to punishment for wrong actions.

The Parable of the Prodigal Son (Luke 15:11-32) teaches what a father's love should be like. And it teaches us about God's unconditional love for us. The father in this parable loved both his sons. He didn't become angry when his younger son decided to take his possessions and leave home. The father's heart was probably broken, but he allowed him to leave.

When the prodigal son finally came to his senses and returned home, he expected to be treated like a servant. But instead he received his father's undeserved love. The father saw his son from a distance, ran to him, threw his arms around him and kissed him! This helps us learn that fathers can hug and kiss their sons! Fathers should be compassionate and tender. The father demonstrated his love by organizing a feast, killing the fattened calf, and putting a ring on his son's finger and sandals on his feet.

When the older son learned of the celebration, he became angry with his father. After all, he had stayed and worked hard all those years for his father. The father did not become angry with this older son either. Instead he said, *"My son, you are always with me and everything I have is yours. But we had to celebrate and be glad, because this brother of yours was dead and is alive again; he was lost and is found"* (Luke 15:31-32, NIV).

Sharing your faith and life with sons and daughters is not a one-time event. It's a lifetime commitment! Pray daily for your children and ask for God's help in meeting their physical, emotional, and spiritual needs. Confess your sins to the Lord. Also confess your sins to your children when you sin against them. Ask the Lord to help you become a better father. Pray that your children will know Christ and that the Word of God will dwell in their hearts. Pray that they will be shielded from dangerous beliefs and practices.

Some of you reading this may feel like a failure. If you are feeling hopeless, bring your hopelessness and concerns to the foot of the cross. There is forgiveness and hope for fathers! Jesus has taken all your sins to the cross—those in the past and even those you committed yesterday and today. Confess yours sins to God and receive His forgiveness. It is new every morning. Then place your hope in Christ! *"God has chosen to make known among the Gentiles the glorious riches of this mystery, which is Christ in you, the hope of glory"* (Colossians 1:27, NIV).

Grandparents—Share Your Faith

"We will not hide them from their children; we will tell the next generation the praiseworthy deeds of the Lord, His power, and the wonders He has done" (Psalm 78:4, NIV). Have you ever noticed that grandparents are often the ones who share their faith with grandchildren? Sometimes parents aren't interested in attending church, reading the Bible, praying, or passing on the faith to the next generation. If you are a grandparent, take heart! You have great influence on the faith life of your grandchildren. Don't take this responsibility lightly!

I recently heard the following story while teaching a Bible study class at a congregation. "I'm active in church and a follower of Jesus because of the love and prayers of my grandmother! When I was young, my grandma took me to church and Sunday school. She read me children's Bible stories. She taught me how to pray. During high school I got involved in drugs and alcohol. I stopped going to church with my grandma. My life went from bad to worse. After I graduated from high school it didn't get better. I went from one dead-end job to another. Then I met my husband. We got married and soon had three children. I loved my husband and children. I knew I was going nowhere fast. I finally asked God to help me clean up my life. I began going to meetings to deal with my addictions. During all those years, my mom didn't help. She'd just scream at me and tell me what a mess I was. But I could always talk with my grandma. I knew she loved me, even though she didn't approve of my lifestyle. Every time I'd visit her she would listen and tell me, 'Kitty, I'm praying for you!' God answered her prayers and mine. Today my husband and I are happily married, we have three great children, and we worship the Lord each week at a local congregation. I'm so glad my grandmother shared her faith with me!"

> I'm active in church and a follower of Jesus because of the love and prayers of my grandmother!

Grandparents, share your faith with your grandchildren! Conversations naturally occur as we read to the grandchildren, travel together, eat and spend time with them. Here are examples of how this might occur:

Four-year-old Annie heard her Sunday school teachers talking about angels. Later she asked her grandfather, "Grandpa, angels helped Jesus when He needed strength in that garden, didn't they? Does God still send angels today to help us?" Grandpa answered, "Wow, what a good question, Annie. Let's take a walk and talk about this some more."

My grandson, Seth, and granddaughter, Lizzy, love to act out Bible stories with me when we visit. We've acted out Mary and Joseph's journey to Bethlehem, the shepherds seeing the star and going to see Jesus, Daniel in the lion's den, Noah and the animals, and much more. After we act the stories out, we talk about the Lord and His Word. Acting the stories out helps Bible stories come alive.

Here are some other suggestions to consider:

1. Read your grandchildren a Bible story that is age-appropriate. ArchBooks are appropriate for children ages 5-9. Read from the Bible itself as well.

2. Give your grandchildren their first children's Bible. Make sure you write a message in it.

3. If your children are not taking their children to church and Sunday school, ask if you can take them. If you live too far away to do this, pray that someone else will invite them to church and Sunday school.

4. Make your grandchildren a part of your daily life. As you bake cookies, ask them to help. As you work in the garden, ask them to help.

5. Take them on nature walks and talk about the Lord and God's beautiful creation of nature. Take a piece of paper and write A through Z down the side of the paper. Then take them to the park and ask them to find something that begins with each letter. For example, an A could be an ant. B could be a bug. C could be a caterpillar. And so on.

6. Invite them to make stamp pad pictures under adult supervision. Begin by having them put their thumbprint on a piece of paper. Then draw a face and stick arms and legs. Explain that God made them unique and special and that their thumbprint is different from every other person's in the world. Then create other animals and

people with thumbprints.

7. Another activity you might try together is potato printing. Carve shapes into potatoes that are cut in half. Then give the potatoes to the children. Allow them to dip them into paint. Print shapes on a large piece of paper or a large brown paper bag. After it dries, use the paper as wrapping paper.

8. Make a fish out of a large paper plate. Cut a large triangle out of the plate. This becomes the mouth of the fish. Put the triangle on the back of the fish as the tail. Then take the fish and sing, "Oh, who can make the fish swim? I'm sure I can't, can you? Oh, who can make the fish swim? No one but God, it's true!"

9. Take your grandchildren camping or, when possible, go on vacation with them.

10. Teach them a song or a game you enjoyed as a child.

11. Talk about your love for God and for them. Tell them Jesus is their Savior and Lord!

12. Pray for them and pray with them.

13. Encourage your children and grandchildren to stand firm in their faith and rely upon the Lord. My husband and I have a living trust that includes a testimony about our faith in Christ. It includes Ephesians 2:8-9 to help our children and grandchildren understand that faith is a free gift and is not dependent upon good works.

Grandchildren, especially young grandchildren, frequently make us laugh. Isn't laughter good for the soul? I thought you might enjoy what eight-year-old children said when they were asked, "What is a grandparent?" Here are some of their responses:

- "Grandparents give us a snack time before bedtime, and say prayers with us. They kiss us even when we've acted badly!"
- "Grandparents are a lady and a man without children of their own. They like other people's children. They like to take walks with us and slow down when we pass flowers, trees, and caterpillars...they never say hurry up!"
- "Grandparents can answer questions like, 'Why isn't God married?'"

- "Everyone should have a grandmother, especially if you don't have TV, because they are the only adults that like to spend time with us."

The following are some of my favorite verses. *"We will not hide them from their children; we will tell the next generation the praiseworthy deeds of the Lord, His power, and the wonders He has done" (Psalm 78:4, NIV). "I am mindful of the sincere faith within you, which first dwelt in your grandmother Lois and your mother Eunice, and I am sure that it is in you as well" (2 Timothy 1:5). "...And that from childhood you have known the sacred writings which are able to give you the wisdom that leads to salvation through faith which is in Christ Jesus" (2 Timothy 3:15).*

Why not say a prayer now and ask the Lord to help you find and use appropriate ways to tell your grandchildren about the praiseworthy deeds of the Lord? You'll be glad you did.

Look—A Newborn Baby!

"Look—a newborn baby! Isn't he precious! How old is he? What's his name?" Have you ever noticed how many people open up and talk to strangers when they see babies or young children? Babies captivate our hearts and give us great joy!

Maybe that's why God the Father sent Jesus, His only begotten Son, into our world as an innocent newborn baby.

The next time you see a newborn baby, consider the awesomeness of our Creator and how He used a baby to restore our relationship with Him. Our sins are forgiven through faith in His Son. Isn't God wonderful? Let's praise His glorious name!

> The next time you see a newborn baby, consider the awesomeness of our Creator and how He used a baby to restore our relationship with Him.

Our family experienced the birth of a grandson in November of 2000. When my husband, Chad, and I first learned we were to be grandparents, our friends and business associates heard all about it. We were excited and happy about the news and looked forward to being grandparents!

I laughed when my husband came home from work a few days after hearing the news. He'd decided to make calls on some of his customers. He'd taken a black magic marker and written, "I'm going to be a grandpa!" on a yellow sticky note and affixed it to his shirt. He wouldn't say anything to the customers, but just waited for them to read the note and watched their reactions. He said it was interesting seeing the many different reactions from, "You're too young to be a grandpa!" "You mean this is your first grandchild? I thought you had lots of grandchildren," to "What's so special about that?" and "Who cares?"

The months went by quickly! Since Coreen and son-in-law, David, lived in Chicago, we heard about the morning sickness, saw the ultrasound pictures through the Internet, helped Coreen select maternity clothes, planned a visit to St. Louis and a baby shower, heard about the active baby that kept her awake during the nights, and finally received the call telling us a son had been born! Three days later we were in Chicago to meet our new grandchild, Seth David Jander. He was beautiful!

Several weeks later, we took some vacation days and traveled again to Chicago for his Baptism. I had forgotten how busy life can be for new parents! It came back quickly! Yes, Seth David Jander is dearly loved and wanted by parents, grandparents, great-grandparents, and aunts and uncles!

But not all babies are wanted! Women who have been encouraged to have an abortion shared the following stories:

- "My mother encouraged me to have an abortion," stated the young mother. "She actually took me to the clinic and dropped me off. I went in, but couldn't go through with it. I eventually married the father of the baby. We're been happily married for six years. I'm so thankful I chose life!"

   She continued, "An interesting thing happened after the baby was born. My mother and my oldest son became best buddies. I never spoke with mom about the fact that she had encouraged me to have an abortion, but I always wondered what she thought about the fact that she would have had a part in the murder of her beloved grandson!"

- "I was adopted after being put in foster care for child abuse. I loved my adoptive parents, but when I got pregnant my father kicked me out. He won't allow me to see my mother or brothers and sisters. I love my son, but wish my adoptive parents would see me and their grandson."

Sad stories! Yet, thousands of young pregnant women find themselves in similar situations. Please pray for women in these situations and support ministries like the Lydia's House, Lutherans for Life, and Our Lady's Inn that offer a place to live during the first few years of their child's life.

Although all babies are not always wanted by their mothers, fathers, and even grandparents, all babies are loved and known by God. *"Before I formed you in the womb I knew you, before you were born I set you apart..." (Jeremiah 1:5a, NIV).*

We must help others learn to celebrate physical, eternal, and the abundant life that God grants us. Celebrate the physical life God gives us! *"Then the Lord God formed man of dust from the ground, and breathed into his nostrils the breath of life; and man became a living being" (Genesis 2:7).* And remember, children are a gift from the Lord!

Celebrate the **eternal life** we have because of our faith in Christ! *"For he who finds me finds life, And obtains favor from the Lord" (Proverbs 8:35). "Just as the Son of Man did not come to be served, but to serve, and*

 *to give His life a ransom for many" (Matthew 20:28). "In Him was life, and the life was the Light of men" (John 1:4). "He who believes in the Son has eternal life" (John 3:36). "Jesus said..., 'I am the bread of life; he who comes to Me will not hunger, and he who believes in me shall never thirst'" (John 6:35). "Jesus said to her, I am the resurrection and the life; he who believes in me will live even if he dies, and everyone*

who lives and believes in Me will never die" (John 11:25-26). Jesus said, *"I am the way, and the truth, and the life; no one comes to the Father, but through Me" (John 14:6).*

Celebrate the **abundant life** that is ours as Christians in God's Kingdom. *"The thief comes only to steal and kill and destroy; I came that they may have life, and have it abundantly" (John 10:10).* You and I can have an abundant life in Jesus Christ. Let's share His love with others!

Media and Our Families

"Mom guess what...!?"

"Kristi, don't bother me now, I'm watching my favorite program."

"But Mom, it's important. I have to tell you what happened."

"I said, not now! Wait until the commercial. Then I'll listen."

* * *

"My favorite movies are slasher films. I like the way people look when they're dead," stated the forth grade girl in an interview by Focus on the Family staff as they did research for "Learn to Discern." Their research found no discernible difference between the favorite television programs and movies of children in public schools and those who attended Christian schools.

* * *

A Michigan State University study group offered a group of four- and five-year-old children the choice of giving up television or giving up their father. One-third of the children said they would give up their fathers. (*Electronic Millstone: Christian Parenting in a Media Age*, p. 56.)

It's a fact! Media affects families, even families in the church! As we work together to reach out with the Gospel, we need to be aware of that influence.

The impact can be positive. Media informs, entertains, stimulates. It provides time for families to be together. It offers the opportunity to see history-in-the-making across the world. When tragedy strikes, it motivates us to respond. Most importantly, media gives us the means to proclaim the precious Gospel of Jesus Christ to a sin-filled world. It offers opportunities to help Christians grow in their faith and understanding of God's Word.

While recognizing these positive aspects of media, we must also be aware of media's negative influences. We need to educate families, especially parents, so they can manage media effectively in their lives and in the lives of their children.

What does research indicate about the effects of media on you and your family? Does a constant diet of profanity, sex, and violence have an effect on Christian beliefs and morals? Does what we view on television impact how we perceive the world we live in? Are we, as Christians, becoming desensitized to situations that the Bible clearly calls sinful?

Beware of the flaming missiles Satan fires at us daily through media! Read Ephesians 6:10-18 with a Christian friend or at the dinner table. Then discuss the following: How can media's influence be a spiritual problem? How has media desensitized you or your children? Finish the following statement: Media programs often make Christians look____. How does the media portrayal of Christians affect our witnessing efforts?

Let's look at some statistics. Do you know the average child watches four hours of television each day and will spend 7.4 years watching television in his or her lifetime?

Excessive television viewing even affects children's physical health. Obesity in children has increased 54 percent over the past 15 years, and doctors report that it is more common in children under 12 who watch television excessively. TV viewing can stifle a child's creativity, reduce reading ability and diminish verbal skills.

"Television violence affects kids in a number of ways. It makes children less able to empathize with the pain and suffering of others," says George Gerbner, a professor at the University of Pennsylvania's Annenberg School for Communication.

There is an average of two murders per night on prime-time television. By the time a child reaches 18, he or she has witnessed 25,000 TV murders. The result is that children are more fearful of the world they live in, accept violence as the solution to problems, and behave aggressively.

In *Who Cares for America's Children?* Urie Broonfenbrenner states: "The primary danger of the television set lies not so much in the behavior it produces—although there is danger there—as the behavior it prevents; the talks, the games, the family festivities and arguments through which much of the child's learning takes place and through which his character is formed. Turning on the television set can turn off the process that transforms children into people."

> When we are watching TV we are not talking, relating to others, enjoying God's creation, or sharing our faith with others.

As you read these statistics notice there are two questions we need to ask about our media consumption. 1) Are the programs we view appropriate for Christians? 2) How much time are we spending passively watching TV? When we are watching TV we are not talking, relating to others, enjoying God's creation, or sharing our faith with others.

The following are suggestions for you and your church group:

1. Ask for God's help to become a better viewer and learn to manage media more effectively within your life. Ask God for forgiveness if you have not used good judgment in your viewing habits. Remember, Jesus died for all your sins, even the sin of viewing inappropriate programs.
2. Educate Christians by offering seminars and programs on managing media within the home through your congregation, school, or Christian organization.
3. Set up a lending library to offer Christians alternatives to prime-time and inappropriate television, cable, DVD, video, and movies. Purchase audio cassettes, books and other literature to learn more about the influence of media on children and families.

Parents should work to alter the viewing habits of their children. Dr. John Frahm has good news for those who become involved in the mitigation process with their children. He stated, "It is important to note when parents become involved in the mitigation process concerning television programs, when they begin to view and discuss programs with their children, all the negative aspects of media viewing can be negated. Media, which is seen as a great evil by many, can actually be used to the benefit of family and society. Mitigation produces improvement in family cohesiveness, communication, academics, and offers parents opportunities to share their faith with their children. But remember, the earlier you begin mitigating within your home the better!"

> Help children choose programs that are appropriate, establish television usage schedules, use television coupons, purchase or rent Christian and family-oriented videos and watch them with your children.

Other suggestions: help children choose programs that are appropriate, establish television usage schedules, use television coupons, purchase or rent Christian- and family-oriented videos and watch them with your children. Consider instituting a once-a-week "no television" night. Plan a family or congregational fun night instead.

Write or telephone the networks when you are unhappy with programs. Call 1-800-251-4039 to obtain a free copy of *The Special Report*

Guide to Family Television Viewing that gives information about where and how to write network leaders.

And finally, *pray* for producers and executives. Pray that God and advertisers will raise up and support Christian producers and writers who will develop Christian programs. Pray that families will learn to use the full armor of God, stand firm against the schemes of the devil (Ephesians 6:10-18), and learn to take up the shield of faith so they can extinguish all the flaming missiles of the evil one!

Although the Bible does not mention the media, television, cable, pod casting, or satellite, it still has words of wisdom for us concerning issues that relate to media. Bible verses you might want to review include: Psalm 101:1-3; Proverbs 3:21; Matthew 18:6; Ephesians 5:1-7; and Philippians 3:9; 4:8.

Media and Outreach

"Bob, I heard the most interesting discussion on the radio tonight when I was driving home from work. I was flipping through the channels when I heard the woman ask, 'Do we know what heaven will be like? Will we know our loved ones?' The host read a description of heaven from the Bible from Revelation 21:10 and 22:5, then they discussed this question. I never knew the Bible had a description of heaven in it! I wonder what else the Bible has to say that might interest me. Becky's been inviting us to her church but I've always said 'No.' Why don't we go with her this weekend? That discussion on the radio sparked my interest. I want to learn more about God and His Word."

How does media affect today's families? Families and those involved in leadership positions within the church need to become aware of the negative influences of media upon themselves, other adults, and children. Then we need to address these issues in a constructive Christ-pleasing way.

Media can also be used to help individuals and their families know, grow, and go for Christ in today's world. It can help families learn to apply faith to life, share God's love and forgiveness, and can often spark interest in those who are unchurched, confused about doctrinal issues, or lukewarm about their faith.

There are many excellent Christian radio and television programs. Unfortunately, many of them address issues that interest the mature Christian. The challenge we face is developing programs that will reach those outside the church.

Why don't we use media opportunities as effectively as we might in today's world? The following are some of my observations:

1) Some church leaders have lost sight of the mission of the church and the meaning of the saving Gospel message.

2) Some leaders are afraid of offending listeners, so they water down the Gospel or use what they refer to as "pre-evangelism." Instead of sharing the saving Gospel message, we hear, "God loves you." This is a true statement, but no one can be saved by hearing that God loves them! Sadly, many have been deceived into thinking this *is* the Gospel. Beware that you are not deceived (Ephesians 4:14)! Instead *"Grow up in all aspects into Him, who is the head, even Christ" (Ephesians 4:15b).*

3) Regrettably, at times, church leaders do not understand the saving Gospel message of Christ. Let me share an example. Several years ago, I had a lengthy conversation with a layman who had been elected as the volunteer president of a small national Christian organization. During our conversation he stated, "I believe my Muslim friends will go to heaven, too." I responded, "Heaven is for those who have faith in Christ. Acts 4:12 states, *'And there is salvation in no one else* [speaking of Christ]*; for there is no other name under heaven that has been given among men by which we must be saved.'"* He countered, "I do not agree that only those who believe in Christ as Savior and Lord will go to heaven!"

   This man was a member of a Lutheran Church—Missouri Synod congregation. It teaches the Gospel correctly. He attended church regularly. But he either did not understand the Gospel or had decided not to believe God's clear Word. Yet he was in charge of a Christian organization! Thankfully, his term ended and a more mature Christian took his place.

4) Lack of financial support is a barrier for Christian ministries and denominations interested in producing and broadcasting media

programs. It is extremely expensive to produce and broadcast quality, innovative programs.

5) Lack of collaboration and cooperation hinders the work of the Body of Christ. Denominational differences often keep us apart. This may be the greatest obstacle facing the church today.

 God has allowed us to develop new technologies in the electronic media field. Satellites, computer networks, teleconferencing, fax machines, long-distance learning, podcasting, Internet Video streaming, and interactive television have changed our world.

Would you join me in praying that God would grant Christian leaders His wisdom and guidance so we may begin to work more cooperatively in proclaiming Christ to the world?

The following story may help illustrate why divisions can have serious eternal consequences.

A group of Christians ventured into a distant country. They were lost and divided over which way they should go to reach civilization. They argued and fought.

"I believe the best way would be to travel through those mountains."

"No. You're wrong. I'm sure the best way is to cross that river."

"You're all wrong. The only way for us to go is to cross the abandoned bridge."

Since no one could agree which way would be the safest route to civilization, they decided to separate. One third chose to climb the treacherous mountains, another third chose to cross the raging river, and the remaining third decided to cross the abandoned bridge. Each group felt its route was the only way to reach civilization and safety.

The first group encountered many hardships. If all three groups had been together, they would have survived, but since two-thirds were not present, there were literally not enough hands to help. The second group, those who chose to cross the turbulent river, also perished. As before, if all had been available, they could have united and survived, but they did not. The third group, those who elected to cross the rickety, abandoned bridge, almost made it. If they would have had more hands, they too would have survived.

Not one of the groups made it to civilization. No one survived and no one was saved! United, cooperating, and working together, any of the three ways could have resulted in the group's eventual success. They would have reached civilization together, but divided they all perished!

A true story? No, of course not. But it could be a modern day parable for the Body of Christ to illustrate how divisions and discord can harm the work of God's Kingdom on earth. Let's stop, look, and listen to each other. Remember, Christ is the head of the church. As believers we are united to Him.

Then remember the story. All three ways could have led to success if the members had worked together, but working separately, all perished.

> Let's unite to utilize media opportunities to expand His Kingdom on earth and bring many into the eternal Kingdom.

What great potential lies before us! Let's unite to utilize media opportunities to expand His Kingdom on earth and bring many into the eternal Kingdom. May God empower us to do this to His glory and through proclamation of His Word!

Everyday Missionaries Share the Good News!

"Chad, you're aware that my dad has cancer. His illness has made me think about what happens when we die. My wife tells me that I need to believe in Jesus, but I'm really confused about all this religious stuff. You know, my parents never attended church. Neither did I. But I really want to know what's going to happen to my father when he dies. And to me! Is this life all there is? It's time that I learn more about God."

My husband, Chad, is one of the best everyday missionaries I know. Recently, while at my sister's for a birthday party, my niece's husband found a quiet corner and asked him to explain more about the Lord. For the first time in his life this man is thinking about what happens after death. He thought God would allow him into heaven if he was good enough. My husband explained that it isn't what we do, but what Jesus Christ has already done for us. He explained that none of us could work our way to heaven. Chad then extended an invitation to join him on an outing to our farm near Bowling Green, Missouri. The trip gave them additional time to talk about critical spiritual issues.

Why did my niece's husband feel comfortable enough to ask my husband such an important question? The answer lies in the fact that Chad had already built a trusting relationship. Building a relationship is an important beginning. And it doesn't have to take a long time. Relationships can be built as we visit with those sitting next to us on an airplane, talk to those in stores and restaurants we frequent, or model our faith to our extended family. As we build relationships, God will open doors of opportunities to share our faith.

> Building a relationship is an important beginning...As we build relationships, God will open doors of opportunities to share our faith!

All Christians are everyday missionaries! As Christ's ambassadors (2 Corinthians 5:20), we model and speak of our faith in the home, church, school, on the job, and in the community. Parents are everyday missionaries as they teach their children to know and love Jesus. Grandparents are everyday missionaries as they pray for their children and grandchildren, assist them, and communicate God's love. Sunday school teachers, vacation Bible school teachers, and youth leaders are also everyday missionaries. Many children who attend Sunday school and vacation Bible school never hear about Jesus in their homes. Teachers in public and Christian schools can also be everyday missionaries.

Everyday missionaries know they are unable to live a perfect life so they confess their sins to the Lord every day. *"If we confess our sins, He is faithful and righteous to forgive us our sins and to cleanse us from all unrighteousness" (1 John 1:9).*

Everyday missionaries pray before they speak. Ask the Lord to grant you His wisdom and to open doors of opportunities to share God's love with those you meet. Pray for God's wisdom and will to be done. Be persistent and fervent in prayer. Pray for the opportunity to share Christ and that God would open doors for the message. And pray that the Lord's message would spread.

Everyday missionaries don't go ahead of the Holy Spirit. Pray for those who are not Christians, but don't move ahead of the Holy Spirit. Wait on the Lord to send you. (Remember, He may send someone else.) Wait for Him to open the door for you to speak. He promises to give us the words we will need in the hour we need them.

Everyday missionaries read and study God's Word. "*All Scripture is inspired by God and profitable for teaching, for reproof, for correction, for training in righteousness; that the man of God may be adequate, equipped for every good work*" *(2 Timothy 3:16-17).*

Sometimes everyday missionaries don't feel equipped to share their faith. They need to become equipped so they can make a defense to everyone who asks. Are you equipped? If not, prayerfully consider how you can grow in your faith. Join a Bible study, study God's word on your own, read daily devotions, and attend a work-shop that will help you learn to share your faith. "*Sanctify Christ as Lord in your hearts, always being ready to make a defense to everyone who asks you to give an account for the hope that is in you, yet with gentleness and reverence*" *(1 Peter 3:15).*

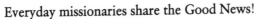

Everyday missionaries share the Good News! Tell those you meet about the Savior who suffered and died for your sins and theirs! Tell them of the Savior who suffered and died for our sins, rose from the dead, and promises eternal life in heaven. "*What was from the beginning, what we have heard, what we have seen with our eyes, what we have looked at and touched with our hands, concerning the Word of Life—and the life was manifested, and we have seen and testify and proclaim to you the eternal life, which was with the Father and was manifested to us...*" *(1 John 1:1-2).*

Going Fishing?

"He said to them, 'Follow Me, and I will make you fishers of men'" (Matthew 4:19).

"Craig, we're going fishing tomorrow morning. Let's get our gear together!" the grandfather told his young grandson. As they prepared for their fishing trip, they chose the appropriate rods and reels, made sure their tackle boxes contained everything they would need, got their clothes ready and made sure they had a variety of bait. Early the next morning they drove to the nearby lake and, just as the sun was rising, pushed their boat onto the lake. "Now let's go catch some fish!" said the grandfather.

To the casual observer, fishing seems quite easy. But those of you who are really into fishing know that catching fish is not as easy as it seems.

 *Fish just don't jump into your boat!* It really takes a lot to catch fish. For example, you don't fish for trout the same way you fish for catfish. So, the first thing you have to decide is what kind of fish you want to catch. Then, depending upon the type of fish you're trying to catch, the appropriate bait must be selected. For instance, really devoted trout fishermen will go as far as studying what kind of insects are in and around a stream they intend to fish. By discovering what types of insects are indigenous to the area, most plentiful, and at what stage of growth the insects are at the time they're fishing, they can then select a fly that most closely resembles the trout's natural food supply for that particular stream at that particular time.

After you've decided what kind of fish you want to catch and what bait you'll be using, the next step is to find a likely spot where the fish might be found. Trout, for instance, will be found just below a ripple in a stream because they feed on insects as the current sweeps them along. Catfish will more than likely be found on the bottom of a lake or river because they're scavengers or "bottom feeders." Bass, on the other hand, are more than likely to be found around fallen trees or areas that provide cover.

Once you've decided where to fish, the real work begins. It takes a lot of practice and skill to "present" accurately and carefully or cast the bait to the spot where, hopefully, the fish are waiting. Then comes the two most difficult aspects of fishing for most people—patiently waiting for a fish to take the bait, and setting the hook.

> Just as fishing for fish requires preparation, knowledge, skill and patience, becoming a *fisher of men* also takes preparation, knowledge, skill, patience, and reliance upon the Lord.

Just as fishing for fish requires preparation, knowledge, skill and patience, becoming a *fisher of men* also takes preparation, knowledge, skill, patience, and reliance upon the Lord. We need to learn how to fish for souls from the Master Fisherman, Jesus Christ. As Jesus' disciples walked and talked with Him for three years before turning the world upside down, we also need to study, listen, and grow in Christ. We should strive to be like the best fisherman the world has ever known—Christ Jesus!

Christ said, *"I will make you fishers of men" (Matthew 4:19).* Matthew 10:19-20 says, *"Do not worry about how or what you are to say; for it will be given you in that hour what you are to say. For it is not you who speak, but it is the Spirit of your Father who speaks in you."*

Are you a fisher of men? Remember, don't wait for fish to jump into your boat! Go into your community and share God's love! Make friends with those who do not know Christ. Be patient with them. Listen and learn about their lives. Show love and concern. Rely on the Holy Spirit to open doors and help you share the Good News. Tell them about the Savior of the world. *"For God so loved the world that He gave His only begotten Son, that whoever believes in Him, shall not perish, but have eternal life" (John 3:16).* So, what are you waiting for? Go fishing!

Part 3

Witnessing During Holidays

Halloween Offers Opportunities to Share Your Faith

Several years ago on Halloween, I was in a fourth grade public school classroom where the children were dressed up for Halloween. Matthew and Eric stand out in my memory.

Matthew was dressed as Moses. He had on a white wig and beard, wore his father's brown robe, a rope belt, and sandles. His parents had carefully cut out cardboard tablets of stone and written the Ten Commandments on them.

I always enjoyed creating Halloween costumes for my children when they were young and remember thinking, "What a great costume. I wish I had thought of it!" Not only was it homemade, but it also gave Matthew an opportunity to share the Word of God with his classmates and teacher in a public school setting.

At the other extreme was Eric, who was dressed as Jason from the movie, "Friday the Thirteenth." His costume was white, his arms were wrapped in white bandages, and he had fake blood smeared across his body. Matthew's costume was very appropriate and in good taste; Eric's was very inappropriate.

I personally see nothing wrong with allowing children to dress up or even go trick-or-treating with parental supervision. There is nothing morally or spiritually wrong with wearing costumes and receiving treats that are willingly given. But costumes should be appropriate and Christ-pleasing. They should not glorify Satan, take the form of wicked or supernatural beings, or hinder our ability to give an effective witness.

You should be aware, however, that Halloween stems from a pagan holiday called Samhain, which is the festival of the dead. It has clear connections with the primitive and sometimes savage rites of the priestly Druids in the pre-Roman, Pre-Christian Celtic communities of Northern and Western Europe, especially in Ireland and Scotland. Because of this primitive festival, the Catholic Church, under Pope Boniface IV in the seventh century, instituted the Christian celebration of All Saints Day on November 1st. Protestants also celebrate the Reformation on October 31st.

Halloween offers us opportunity to share our faith in Christ with children and their parents. Prayerfully consider how you and your family can reach out with God's love during any Halloween season. Here are two suggestions to consider:

1. When trick-or-treaters arrive at your door, place candy and a Christian Halloween tract in their sack. Or, wrap the candy you give them in sacks with a Christian message. These tracts and sacks can tell the children and their parents about Jesus, the Savior of the world, and can extend an invitation to visit your congregation. Information about Halloween tracts and sacks with a Christian message are available at Concordia Publishing House (1-800-325-3040 or www.cph.org/cphstore).

2. Consider organizing an alternative Halloween party at your school or congregation for your own children and for those within your neighborhood.

Years ago, while I was the executive director of the National Lutheran Parent-Teacher League, St. Mark's Lutheran Church and School in Eureka, Missouri, submitted the following Halloween alternative program to us. It is shared as a sample of what your congregation, church group, or school could do for your families and friends.

The event was entitled "A Night on Noah's Ark." Its purpose was to provide an alternative to Halloween celebrations that the world promotes and to substitute a celebration with a Christian emphasis for children and families to attend.

It was initiated by the Board of Evangelism at St. Mark's, but involved many other groups as well. Three couples were asked to chair it. The target group was age three through those in sixth grade. The Sunday school and the Christian day school were the prime groups who were encouraged to attend. It was marketed to families with children. It was advertised in the church and neighborhood newspapers. Flyers were sent home with school children.

The children from St. Mark's were encouraged to invite friends and relatives and encouraged to dress up as animals that would have been on Noah's Ark. And, of course, Noah was also present. A family supper was served at 5:30 p.m. with Noah leading the animals onto the ark as the doors opened at 6:15 p.m.

Inside the ark were 10 different booths where games and activities were set up, separated by bales of hay for the animals. As the children came, each was given a shopping bag with candy in it which served as a prize.

Ten "animals" were led to each booth. When the event at that booth was complete, they would go to the next booth, rotating around the gym until all the games had been played. They could return to their booth of choice once the rounds had been made. The adults in each booth also dressed up to add to the ark atmosphere.

Booth ideas included:

Ring Toss	Fill 10 two-liter bottles with water and line them up like bowling pins. Have the children try to throw rubber rings over them to win a prize.
Bean Bag Toss	Draw an animal on a large poster board. Make the mouth wide open and cut it out. The children try to toss bean bags into the animal's mouth. Those that do win a prize.
Cupcake Walk	Tape colored squares to the floor. Children walk around the circle when the music begins. When the music stops, those standing on certain colors are winners. Each winner receives a cupcake wrapped in a plastic bag.

Sucker Pull	Children pull a sucker out of cardboard base. Those who select suckers with colored ends receive a prize. Everyone keeps their sucker.
Apple Roll Relay Races	Two children race to roll the apple with their hand across the floor to the finish line.
Puppet Show	Children sit on bales of hay to watch. The puppet shows have a Christian message.
Pumpkin Story-teller	There are two pumpkins. One is shriveled and carved; one is still good. The story is about sin and the need for Jesus' forgiveness.
Fish Pond	Children put in a pole with a line attached and pull out a prize.

Christian prizes were used. To obtain small Christian gifts, watch for sales at Christian book stores, the Concordia Publishing House (www.cph.com) or try www.orientaltrading.com. Everyone got a prize at each booth whether they won or not.

It was a fun-filled Christian evening. At 7:30 p.m. the program was closed with a short devotion in the center of the ark. Bales of hay with stuffed animals sitting around were in the center where Noah led the devotion and singing. A rainbow was raised (a pole with colorful streamers) at the conclusion of the devotional. The subject of the closing devotion was on God's promises.

Yes, Halloween offers us an opportunity to witness! Join me in praying that Christians will seek ways to share their faith and the wonderful works of the Lord during the Halloween season!

Thankful for Faith, Family, and Life

Why are you thankful for faith, family, and life? For one of our special Thanksgiving *Family Shield* radio broadcasts, we invited a three-year-old, a sixth grader, and several adults to share why they were thankful for faith, family, and life. I hope their words will be a blessing to you and that you will consider how you can share your faith with family and friends during the Thanksgiving holidays.

> **Irena, a 3-year old:** "I'm thankful for my toys, my lamb, my bed, my mom, my grandma, and friends. My lamb plays 'Jesus Loves Me'; want to hear me sing it?"

Are you thankful for your children? Your grandchildren? The children you teach? Why not tell them?

> **Carol, Irena's mom:** "I'm thankful God finally opened the door for me to adopt Irena from the USSR. She is such a blessing!
>
>
>
> "I'm especially thankful to God for life and today's wonderful technology. I've always told the Lord I'd go to be with Him anytime, but this year when I learned I needed a heart operation, I realized how much I wanted to stay around and raise Irena. God brought me through the surgery and has richly blessed me! I'm certainly thankful for life!
>
> "The Lord made me and Irena a family in His own good time. Kay, encourage your readers and listeners to give God a chance! Sometimes when God answers our prayers with 'wait' we give up. Allow God time to perform miracles in your life. Sometimes we need to be willing to take a risk for God."

> **Stephen, a sixth grader:** "I'm thankful for my mom and dad. They love and care for me. I'm thankful for my friends and for soccer. I love soccer! And most of the time I'm thankful for my older brother and sister."

I asked Stephen how he puts his faith into action. He said, "I try to act like a Christian instead of being mean or calling others names. I try to be kind when others are unkind. I try not to put others down."

> **Bill, Stephen's father:** "I'm thankful for my wife and three children.

Our faith in the Lord and each other keeps us together. We strive to live by biblical principles.

"Difficult times will arise in everyone's life. Things have been tough for us, but God continues to walk with us through these trying times. We continue to keep our eyes focused on Him. I've been strengthened through my faith and my family."

> Difficult times will arise in everyone's life. Things have been tough for us, but God continues to walk with us through these trying times. We continue to keep our eyes focused on Him.

Mike McHardy: "I'm thankful to the Lord for allowing me to serve Him as the General Manager of KSIV AM and FM in St. Louis, Missouri. I'm grateful to Him for allowing these stations to be used for His Kingdom. KSIV is touching families through programs like *Family Shield*. KSIV is about programs and people. I'm grateful for both."

Jim Day: "I'm thankful to the Lord Jesus Christ for allowing me to serve Him and His people through the *St. Louis Metro Voice*. The newspaper is dedicated to uniting the Christian community and providing useful information they may not read anywhere else.

"The Bible says we perish for the lack of knowledge. Christians need to be informed. The secular media only covers part of the story. God has given me the responsibility to provide additional information to St. Louis readers. I would like to wish your listeners and our readers a blessed Thanksgiving holiday. Always keep in mind where the gifts come from!"

Tim Barrends: "I'm thankful for the Christian upbringing of my parents. I remember the devotions and prayers we'd have for missionary families. We had pictures of them to remind us to pray for them.

"You know, Kay, one sign of the last days is that people will not be thankful. Christians need to be thankful! I believe anything we get outside of salvation is a bonus from God. Thank the Lord for prayers that are answered! Praise and thank Him for the gifts

He gives us!

"Someone once said the best antidote for mental illness is an attitude of gratitude! Remind your listeners and readers to be sensitive to the needs of those around them. Pray with others. Tell others how God has blessed you!"

Cookie Brauer: "Besides being thankful for my faith and family, I'm also thankful for men like Steve Cohen of *Apple of His Eye Mission Society* who are taking the Gospel to our Jewish friends. We should also be thankful to moms who make cookies, for grandmas who read books, for dads who coach Little League after a long day at work, and for teachers who stay after school and help us learn. I'm thankful for radio stations like KSIV, where we hear the Gospel and God's Word proclaimed. I'd encourage your listeners and readers to list reasons they are thankful."

Kay Meyer: "I'm thankful, too. I'm thankful for the opportunity to share God's love through the ministry and my monthly column in the *St. Louis Metro Voice* and for the many opportunities to share and equip families through the Gospel and God's Word."

"I'm thankful that the Lord loved me enough to suffer and die for me and for the forgiveness that is new every morning. I'm thankful for my husband, Chad, my three children, my son-in-law, and our beautiful grandchildren."

Why are you thankful for faith, family, and life? Why not spend time praising and thanking God for the blessings He bestows upon you and your family? Then consider how you can share His love with others during the holiday season.

"*Amen, blessing and glory and wisdom and thanksgiving and honor and power and might, be to our God forever and ever Amen*" (Revelation 7:12).

Share Your Faith During the Holidays

We couldn't wait to tell the shoppers about the greatest gift of all...Jesus, the Savior of the world! Several years ago, members of St Mark's Lutheran Church in Eureka, Missouri, used the Saturday before Christmas to witness within their community in a unique way. The local Wal-Mart gave them permission to have a gift-wrapping table in the storefront. As shoppers entered the store, they were handed a tract that said, "Two free gifts for you."

The first message was simple: "Our greatest Christmas gift is from God. He sent His only Son, Jesus Christ, and grants us forgiveness and eternal life. And, His gift is free!"

The second was that shoppers could have one Christmas gift wrapped free as they left the store. While shoppers waited to have their gift wrapped, they were a captive audience for church volunteers who were  wrapping their presents. Many shoppers tried to give a donation. That just made the "free gift" message concerning Jesus even more meaningful to share!

More than 500 tracts were given away. Over 100 gifts were wrapped with holiday paper, ribbons, and name tags donated by members of St. Mark's. Volunteers reported that the two-hour shifts went quickly and that it was fun to watch the reactions of shoppers.

As this congregation demonstrated through their innovative gift-wrapping program, the holiday season can offer us unique opportunities to share our faith.

Have you considered how you will share your faith during Thanksgiving and Christmas?

Here are some suggestions for you to consider:
- Invite someone who might spend the holiday alone to your Thanksgiving celebration. As you gather to enjoy the meal, ask each person to share why he or she is thankful to God. Witnessing opportunities abound as you thank God for sending His Son, for the forgiveness of sins, eternal life, for daily bread, and for family and friends.
- Select and send holiday cards that share a Christian message.

Thanksgiving cards can focus on God's blessing and gifts (Matthew 6:11, 18-25). Christmas cards should focus on Jesus as the Savior of the world (Luke 2:11).

- Sometime back, a participant in a parenting class told me her family prays for each person or family who sends them a Christmas card on the day it arrives. What a great idea!
- Do you include a form letter with your Christmas card? Why not add at least one paragraph about what Christ means to you? Don't just talk about church issues, talk about your relationship with Christ.
- Some use the money they would normally spend on Christmas cards and give it to their favorite ministry.
- Purchase holiday tracts and enclose them with cards and bills during the holiday season.
- Wear a Thanksgiving or Christmas button. Buttons that say "Jesus Is the Reason for the Season" present a message that can't be missed and may open up opportunities to share your faith verbally.
- Invite an unchurched person to attend a Thanksgiving or Christmas event at your church. Children's programs offer a wonderful opportunity to invite relatives and close friends.
- Bake and deliver Christmas cookies or homemade bread to a shut-in from your congregation or a new neighbor. Stay and visit.
- Gather a group of friends and sing Christmas carols at a nearby nursing home. Stay and read the Bible or pray with someone who doesn't receive regular family visits.
- Don't forget to share your faith within your own family. Begin a family tradition by reading the Christmas story to your children on Christmas Eve or Christmas morning. Two appropriate readings include Luke 2:1-20 or Matthew 1:18—2:15.
- The Christmas season is a wonderful time to begin devotions within the home. Children love to light candles and read the Bible verses. Remind them that Jesus is the light of the world (John 8:12).
- Plan games, serve inexpensive snacks, and close with a short devotion. Devotional time might include a series of questions the children can help you answer, along with appropriate Bible verses. Some suggestions include: "Why do you think God put the star in

the sky?" Talk about how it led the wise men to the Christ Child. "Why do you think it shined so brightly?" Talk about Jesus being the light of the world and how He lights our path. Ask the children how Jesus was wrapped up. Explain that swaddling clothes were used during Biblical times and why they were used. Ask, "How could this relate to why we wrap presents today? What gifts did the wise men bring Jesus? How does God protect us from danger?" Close with a prayer.

As these suggestions demonstrate, there are myriad ways to share our faith. Consider how you might do this during the holiday season.

Then, join me, as well as my family and thousands of other Christians throughout the world in praising our Wonderful Counselor, the Prince of Peace, and the Savior of the World! He is worthy of all our praise and adoration!

"For to us a child is born, to us a son is given, and the government will be on his shoulders. And he will be called Wonderful Counselor, Mighty God, Everlasting Father, Prince of Peace" (Isaiah 9:6, NIV).

Christmas—A Time to Share Our Faith with Family and Friends

"The virgin will be with child and will give birth to a son, and they will call him Immanuel" – which means, *"God with us"* (Matthew 1:23, NIV). Yes, Christmas is a time to remember the birth of God's only begotten Son, Jesus Christ, and to worship Him.

The holiday season is also a time to share our faith with family and friends. Following are some ideas to help celebrate the holiday season and share your faith.

Organize a Birthday Celebration for Jesus. Invite several families and friends to a birthday celebration for Jesus at your home or congregation.

Ask those who attend to bring an unwrapped gift that will be donated to a prisoner's child, a seminary student's child, or another Christian ministry that gives gifts to children during the holidays.

Why not create your own wrapping paper at your celebration? Using butcher block paper, do potato printing or decorate the wrapping paper with fingerprint art using a stamp pad. Magic markers and crayons can also be used. Encourage families and groups to work together.

After you've completed the wrapping paper, invite guests to create a homemade card to put inside their gift. Remind them that the child who receives the gift may not know the Lord. Think about ways your card can communicate God's love.

The following games, activities, and mixers may be used during the birthday celebration or at other times during the holiday season.

Bible Charades. This was a favorite Bible activity in our home when our three children were growing up. You can play Bible charades with your family and friends. On slips of paper, write several titles of Bible stories that can be acted out, such as: Mary and Joseph travel to Jerusalem, the Magi follow the star, the angels announce Christ's birth to the shepherds, Moses brings the 10 Commandments down from Mt. Sinai, Noah builds the ark, Jonah runs away from God, Elijah and the prophets of Baal, Jesus feeds the 5,000, Joseph and the coat of many colors, Judas betrays Jesus in the garden, and Jesus appears to Thomas. Put the slips of paper into an envelope. Divide your family or group into two teams. Let one team select a slip with a story on it. Encourage them to use as many members of their team as possible in acting out the story. The other team tries to guess which story they are acting out.

A Mixer. In advance, select a holiday theme or phrase like "Merry Christmas" or "Happy Holidays." Write one letter of your theme or phrase on small paper bags. You might select "Happy Holidays." On the first paper bag you would write a large "H." After you have written letters on all the bags, begin to search your home for items that begin with the letter on the bags. Inside the

"H" bag you might put a small play "house" from your children's toy chest, a hairpin, or a handkerchief. The next letter is "A." You might put an apple into this bag. Then look for items that begin with "P" until all the bags have items in them. Staple or tape the bags shut.

To play the game, hand out the bags to various individuals in the group. Then give each participant a piece of paper with the phase "Happy Holidays" written on it.

HAPPY HOLIDAYS

What is it?   Think of a way this item relates to your faith.
   1. H =
   2. A =
   3. P =
   4. P =
   5. Y =

And so on...

Tell participants they are to guess what's in the bags and write it on their paper. Explain that the items in the bag begin with the letter on each bag. You can have everyone work independently, but it's more fun to assign teams to work together. You can also help the younger children participate by using groups. Include one or two difficult or funny items in the bags. The "A" could be air, so there would not be anything in the bag. After everyone's had time to guess what's in the bags, open them up and see which team had the most correct answers. Have small prizes like candy bars or sticks of gum.

The challenge question comes last. Ask each group to think of a way each item relates to their faith. This can often be very difficult! At times they may not be able to think of anything. Encourage them to think creatively. A house might remind them that God supplies all their daily needs, an apple might remind them that they are the apple of God's eye, and so on.

Make Play Dough. *How to make play dough.* To make the play dough, mix one cup of flour, one-half cup of table salt, one cup of water, one teaspoon powered alum, two tablespoons of cream tartar, one tablespoon vegetable or canola oil, and several drops of food coloring in a metal pan.

Heat over medium heat for five minutes or until the mixture thickens. Stir constantly. Remove from heat and let cool. After it's cool, wrap it in plastic wrap or a zipper plastic bag and place in the refrigerator.

Using the play dough. Young children love to punch and roll the play dough. Allow them to experiment. You might make pretend foods. Suggestions include chocolate chip cookies. Roll small circles. Let your child press the circles flat. Then take tiny pieces of play dough and make tiny circles. Place these circles on the flattened cookie to represent the chocolate chips. Other pretend foods that are easy to make include a hot dog, a hamburger, and a pizza.

You might make animals. Snakes are easy for young children. Other animals include turtles, dogs, or cats.

During the holidays you could make a wreath, a Christmas tree, a star—or use Christmas cookie cutters.

As you play with the play dough together, take time to discuss your faith. Show your child how to make a hand print in the play dough. Explain that God made each of us unique and special and that every person has different fingerprints. Tell them how much God loves them. Tell them how much you love them.

Help them roll two long narrow pieces of play dough and put them together to form a cross. Remind them that Jesus died on the cross to take away our sins and give us eternal life.

Finger Paint with Shaving Cream. Sit with your children at a waterproof table and spray a small ball (about the size of a very small lemon) of shaving cream on the table for each one. Show your children how to spread it around using different parts of their hands and fingers. Encourage them to use the palm of their hand, tips of their fingers, and the sides of their hand or fingers to create different patterns.

Younger children like to make circles. Show older children how to write the letters of their name, or draw a square, cross, triangle, tree, or house. Encourage them to be creative and design their own unique pattern.

Make a large cross together. Tell the children about Jesus who is the Savior of the world. Before long the shaving cream will begin to evaporate. This gives you the opportunity to discuss a new word with them – "evaporation."

Make a Snack Together. Children love to cook! Christmas is a great time to make Christmas cookies, decorate cupcakes, or make Rice Krispie treats together.

Conclude the Evening with a Prayer. Remember to thank God for His unending love and forgiveness in Jesus. Also thank Him for your family and the good time you have had together.

A New Year's Resolution

May your New Year be filled with the joy and peace that only the Savior can bring! Many people make a New Year's resolution annually. One resolution that every Christian should make is to share their faith more often.

Begin by praying that God will open doors of opportunity for you to share your faith in Christ with family members, friends, co-workers and those you meet in the community. Ask God to give you the words in the hour that you need them.

"But when they hand you over, do not worry about how or what you are to say; for it will be given you in that hour what you are to say. For it is not you who speak, but it is the Spirit of your Father who speaks in you" (Matthew 10:19-20).

God regularly opens doors of opportunity for me. Let me share one opportunity that might help you see how simple witnessing can be when you rely upon the Lord.

A few years ago I searched for and found a new hairdresser. My former hairdresser had retired. A few weeks later I broke my wrist. Because I couldn't wash my hair without great difficulty, I began making a weekly visit to the beauty parlor.

Kim and I began to build a relationship as we talked each week. She is a really lovely young woman with two teenage daughters. I enjoyed learning about her family. She also learned about my husband, three children, and our beloved grandchildren. From our conversations I realized she wasn't a Christian. She did, however, believe in living a moral life.

I began praying for God to open a door for me to share my faith with her. After several weeks, she asked about my work. I explained that Family Shield Ministries was an outreach and equipping ministry. I mentioned that we were Lutheran. When I mentioned this, she asked, "What's the difference between Lutherans and Catholics?" She went on to explain that her husband was Catholic, but she didn't attend church. She thought the Catholic Church and the Lutheran Church were different religions, but I explained that they were the same religion (Christianity), but different denominations. I then shared some similarities and differences.

> Sharing our faith doesn't need to be difficult.

She then asked, "Does someone have to be baptized to go to heaven?" I answered, "No, the thief on the cross wasn't baptized, but Jesus promised him that he would be with Him in paradise or heaven." She responded, "My mother-in-law is Catholic and she says that I'm going to go to hell because I'm not baptized." This comment opened the door for me to share the Law and Gospel and to explain what it means to have faith in Christ. I also explained why God grants us eternal life. Kim continues to ask questions about God's Word and her eternal life. Please keep her in your prayers.

Sharing our faith doesn't need to be difficult. I frequently teach workshops and Bible studies entitled: "Witnessing—A Lifestyle." Some of the points I use and discuss in my presentation include:

- Begin with prayer.
- Build a relationship.
- Share a personal testimony and relate faith to life issues.
- Listen, show concern, and respond to needs.
- Share the Law and Gospel.

One of the most common schemes of Satan is to confuse people into thinking they are going to heaven because they are good. We need to help people understand that the Bible says keeping the Law can't save us. *"Because by the works of the Law no flesh will be justified in His sight; for through the Law comes the knowledge of sin" (Romans 3:20).*

The Bible also tells us that we are all sinners. *"For all have sinned and fall short of the glory of God, being justified as a gift by His grace through the redemption which is in Christ Jesus" (Romans 3:23).* We are saved by faith, not works! *"For by grace you have been saved through faith; and that not of yourselves, it is the gift of God; not as a result of works, that no one may boast" (Ephesians 2:8-9).*

We need to point people to the Savior. *"For God so loved the world, that He gave His only begotten Son, that whoever believes in Him shall not perish, but have eternal life" (John 3:16).*

We need to proclaim the saving Gospel. *"Now I make known to you, brethren, the gospel which I preached to you, which also you received, in which also you stand, by which also you are saved, if you hold fast the word which I preached to you, unless you believed in vain. For I delivered to you as of first importance what I also received, that Christ died for our sins according to the Scriptures and that He was buried, and that He was raised on the third day according to the Scriptures and that He appeared to Cephas [Peter], then to the twelve. After that He appeared to more than five hundred brethren at one time, most of whom remain until now, but some have fallen asleep; then He appeared to James, then to all the apostles; and last of all, as to one untimely born, He appeared to me also" (1 Corinthians 15:1-8).*

Paul and Silas witnessed to prisoners and jailers. *"But about midnight Paul and Silas were praying and singing hymns of praise to God, and the prisoners were listening to them; and suddenly there came a great earthquake, so that the foundations of the prison house were shaken; and immediately all the doors were opened and everyone's chains were unfastened... and after he brought them out, the jailer asked, 'Sirs, what must I do to be saved?' They said, 'Believe in the Lord Jesus, and you will be saved, you and your household.' And they spoke the word of the Lord to him together with all who were in his house. And he took them that very hour of the*

night and washed their wounds, and immediately he was baptized, he and all his household" (Acts 16:25-26, 30-33).

The apostle John proclaims the Word of Life in 1 John. "*What was from the beginning, what we have heard, what we have seen with our eyes, what we have looked at and touched with our hands, concerning the Word of Life—and the life was manifested, and we have seen and testify and proclaim to you the eternal life, which was with the Father and was manifested to us*" (1 John 1:1-2).

So, as the New Year again comes upon us, make a New Year's resolution to share your faith. "*But sanctify Christ as Lord in your heart, always being ready to make a defense to everyone who asks you to give an account for the hope that is in you, yet with gentleness and reverence*" (1 Peter 3:15).

God Has a Great Big Heart!

Valentine's Day arrives each year on February 14th. The stores are full of pink and red hearts that remind us to select that special card, box of candy, or gift for our husband, wife, children or loved one.

Have you ever wondered where the tradition of Valentine's Day came from? Here's one tradition. It is said that Valentino was a kind and well-loved monk who lived in the second century. One day a decree was made by the Roman Emperor that anyone who worshipped any gods other than those he believed in would be put to death.

Valentino said with conviction, "I will worship no one but Jesus Christ."

He was warned if he refused to worship the emperor's gods he would go to the gallows. Valentino replied, "I'm willing to die for my Savior who died for me."

So, because Valentino wouldn't worship false gods, he was put into prison. One of the jailers who guarded him had a blind daughter named Julia. He got to know and like Valentino. Knowing Valentino was educated, he asked him if he would teach his daughter math, history, and geography. Valentino said "Yes." One day Julia asked, "Do you believe in prayer, Valentino?" He replied, "Oh, yes, I believe in prayer and in the God who answers prayer."

She said, "Then would you join me in praying that God would heal my eyesight." They prayed together. God performed a miracle and healed her blindness.

It is said that shortly after this wonderful miracle of God, Valentino was put to death. He died on February 14, 270 AD. Sadness overcame the people because so many knew him as a kind, loving monk who loved God. A tree was planted over his grave. Every year on the anniversary of his death people would come and leave a small gift to remember St. Valentino. Why? Because he was a man who had a great big heart!

God loves us with an everlasting love that transcends time and space.

We don't know if this story is true, but we do know that God has a great big heart! He is worthy of our praise and adoration. God loves us with an everlasting love that transcends time and space. So many people today are seeking love in all the wrong places. Only God's love will last forever!

So, as we think about Valentine's Day—a day to remember to tell those we care about how much we love them—, as we see the hearts that remind us that Valentine's Day will be here soon, let's also remember God's love and share His love with others!

Why share God's love? Because God loved us first! Someone has defined love as giving. God gave us His Son Jesus Christ to demonstrate His love toward us. *"In this is love, not that we loved God, but that He loved us and sent His Son to be the propitiation for our sins" (1 John 4:10). "See how great a love the Father has bestowed upon us, that we would be called children of God; and such we are" (1 John 3:1a).*

We only have one word for love in the English language, but in the Greek language there are three words for love. *Agape* is the Greek word that describes God's unconditional and undeserving love. The other two Greek words are *eros*, which is the physical love of a husband and wife, and *phileo*, which describes the love people have for relatives or close friends.

As we meditate upon God's love for us, the Holy Spirit can help us share His love with others. *"Do not worry about what to say or how to say it. At that time you will be given what to say, for it will not be you speaking, but the Spirit of your Father speaking through you" (Matthew 10:19-20, NIV). "For God so loved the world that He gave His only begotten Son that whosoever believes in Him shall not perish but have eternal life" (John 3:16).*

Need some ideas for sharing God's love at Valentine's Day? Here are some ideas:

1) Buy a Christian book, video, Bible, or audiocassette to give to a loved one. Why not consider *501 Practical Ways to Love Your Wife and Kids* or *Celebrating Life as Grandparents* by Rev. Roger Sonnenberg (available from Concordia Publishing House)?

2) Make or buy a Valentine's Day card with a Christian message. Add a Bible verse about God's love and forgiveness on the card you give.

3) Write a letter and tell a loved one why you are thankful to God for his or her love and support.

4) Invite those you care about to a Bible study, worship service, or special church event.

Don't let your love grow cold! Matthew 24:12 states that one of the signs of the end of time will be that the love of most will grow cold. Satan wants to change real self-sacrificing love into self-indulgent love.

"Keep yourself in God's love as you wait for the mercy of our Lord Jesus Christ to bring you to eternal life. Be merciful to those who doubt; snatch others from the fire and save them; to others show mercy, mixed with fear —hating even the clothing stained by corrupt flesh. To him who is able to keep you from falling and to present you before his glorious presence without fault and with great joy—to the only God our Savior be glory, majesty, power and authority, through Jesus Christ our Lord, before all ages, now and forevermore! Amen" (Jude 21-25, NIV).

Easter Offers Opportunities to Share Christ

The stores are full of brightly colored Easter baskets, chocolate bunnies, marshmallow eggs, and beautiful clothes! Lenten services are being held at area congregations. Easter is near. How can we use traditional Easter activities to share our faith with those in our families? Although most Christians understand that Easter is about the death and resurrection of Jesus Christ, the secular world promotes it as just another holiday. Yet, the Bible tells us to take every opportunity to tell others about our Savior. The following are suggestions for using Easter activities to share Christ.

Devotional Resurrection Eggs. Twelve large plastic eggs can be used as a teaching tool for children and adults of all ages. Inside each colored egg place a small item that reminds us of the passion story along with a written Bible verse. (Parents may want to prepare by reading the Easter story.) Note items that you might use. Put an empty communion cup or small piece of unleavened bread inside one egg. These remind us of the Last Supper meal (Luke 22:17-20). In another egg put a small sponge and the Bible verse about how Jesus' enemies gave Him a sponge filled with vinegar when He was thirsty. In another egg put a piece of wood. As you open this egg talk about how Jesus was nailed to the cross and suffered for our sins. In another egg you might put a toothpick that represents the spear that went into Jesus' side after His death. An eraser inside an egg can help

children understand that with faith in Christ their sins are forgiven and washed away (or erased). Another egg could have a coin inside. Judas betrayed Jesus with 30 pieces of silver. What about the number 12? Ask how the 12 eggs remind them of the story of Jesus' birth, suffering, and death. Hopefully, they will remember that Jesus selected 12 disciples or apostles. A small chain can be used to explain how we are in bondage to sin before Jesus broke the chains by His life, death, and resurrection. A piece of linen can remind us that they stripped Jesus and beat Him. A thorn can remind us of the crown of thorns he wore. The final egg that you open should be empty. The disciples found an empty tomb! Once you've decided on what to put inside the eggs and the appropriate Bible verse, arrange the eggs in the order of the Gospel story. Then open one egg each day for 12 days before Easter.

Dye Eggs with Natural Items. When my children were young, one year we dyed Easter eggs using a variety of natural products. Eggs boiled in onion skins turn yellow/orange. Eggs boiled with blueberries make a beautiful color. Beets also make a great color. After boiling the eggs, you can fix the beets as a vegetable. Spinach leaves are another option. Experiment with various vegetables and fruits. Use these times to talk about the wonderful world God created and how nature can be used to show us a rainbow of colors.

Hunt for the Easter Basket. Do you put out Easter baskets for the children to find on Easter morning? Why not adapt this tradition and allow the children to hunt for baskets on Easter morning? After they have ample time to find their basket and look at what's inside, invite them to sit with you as you read a portion of the Easter story together. You might purchase a book about the Easter story that is age appropriate or read it from their Bible. One of my favorite stories after hunting for the baskets was to read the story of the women running to tell the disciples that Jesus was not there and how two disciples ran to the tomb looking for Jesus. Jesus was no longer in the tomb. He had risen from the grave!

Act Out the Easter Story. Another good activity is to act out the Easter story. You can do this with your children or involve the extended family at your gathering. Stories from the Bible can come alive as children and adults act them out and discuss them together.

Easter Egg Hunts. Many congregations organize an Easter Egg Hunt and invite their community. Use this opportunity to extend an invitation to those who come to join you for services. Make sure people receive something in print about the times of services.

Before you send the children to hunt for the eggs, share the Easter story. Make it a mini children's sermon. Explain that after the resurrection the disciples hunted for Jesus, but He was no longer in the grave. He had risen from the dead! Tell them that when we have faith in Jesus, our sins are forgiven. When we die we will go to heaven to be with Jesus.

Easter Cookies. Making Easter cookies can become a family tradition. You need: one cup whole pecans, one tsp. vinegar, three egg whites, a pinch of salt, one cup sugar, a plastic zipper bag, a wooden spoon, tape, and a Bible. Preheat the oven to 300 degrees F.

Place pecans in a zipper bag and allow each member of the family to beat them with the wooden spoon. Soon they will break into small pieces. Remind them that when Jesus was arrested, He was beaten by the soldiers.

Make sure you tell them that He was beaten for their sins and your sins!

Let each child smell the vinegar. Put it into the mixing bowl. Tell them that when Jesus was on the cross and was thirsty, He was given vinegar to drink from a sponge. Read John 19:28-30 together.

Add egg whites to the vinegar. Eggs represent life. Explain that Jesus gave His life to give us forgiveness and life everlasting. Read John 10:10-11 together.

Sprinkle a little salt into each person's hand. Let them taste it and brush the rest into the bowl. Explain that this can represent the salty tears shed by Jesus' followers and the bitterness of our own sin. Read Luke 23:27 together.

Now add one cup of sugar. Explain that the sweetest part of the Easter story is that Jesus died because He loves us. He wants us to know and love Him. Read John 3:16.

Beat with a mixer on high for 13 minutes or until stiff peaks form. Explain that the color white represents purity. Our sins are washed away and

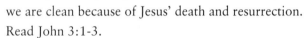

we are clean because of Jesus' death and resurrection. Read John 3:1-3.

Fold in the broken nuts. Drop spoonsful of dough onto wax paper on a cookie sheet. Explain that each cookie represents the rocky tomb where Jesus' body was laid after His death. Read Matthew 27:57-60.

Put the cookie sheet into the oven, close the door and turn the oven OFF. Give everyone a piece of tape and seal the oven door. Explain that Jesus' tomb was sealed. Read Matthew 27:65-66.

GO TO BED!

First say that we might be sad to leave the cookies in the oven. The disciples were sad when Jesus was placed into the tomb. Read John 16:20 and 22.

On Easter morning, open the oven and give everyone a cookie. Notice the cracked surface and take a bite. The cookies are hollow! On the first Easter Jesus' followers found the tomb open and empty! Read Matthew 28:1-9 together.

Family Get-Togethers. Extended families gather together for food and fellowship on Easter. If your family is like ours, some of your relatives are not Christians or have fallen away from the church. Use these opportunities to be light and salt to your loved ones. Talk about the sermon your pastor preached that morning. Talk about Jesus' resurrection and that He still lives.

"Jesus said to him [Thomas], *'Because you have seen Me, have you believed? Blessed are they who did not see, and yet believed'" (John 20:29).*

Part 4

Witnessing in the Community, Congregations and Schools

---●---

"Go therefore and make disciples of all the nations, baptizing them in the name of the Father and the Son and the Holy Spirit, teaching them to observe all that I commanded you; and lo, I am with you always, even to the end of the age" (Matthew 28:19-20).

---●---

Sharing the Gospel

I was at a local beauty parlor, and my beautician and I were discussing our respective churches.

"Does your church preach the Gospel?" I asked.

"Oh, yes," she responded, "but we also read from the Old Testament."

With a shock, I realized, "She thinks I'm speaking about the Gospel writers and their books, Matthew, Mark, Luke, and John!"

Some years ago while I was an employee at Lutheran Hour Ministries, I led a Bible study. During the study the question arose, "What's the Gospel?" There was some confusion among the participants concerning what we meant by the Gospel. Participants were asked to do a survey and ask several relatives, co-workers, and neighbors the question, "What's the Gospel?"

We received various answers including: "It's God's Word...and every word in it." "God loves us." "I have no idea." "It is the gospels (Matthew, Mark, Luke and John)." Some even said, "It means we have to obey God's laws." This simple survey demonstrated the confusion many have about the saving Gospel message.

Often there is confusion when we say, "Let's share the Gospel." Most have heard the term "The Gospel," but don't always understand its meaning.

The "Gospel" is Greek for "Good News" and tells us how we can be saved from our sins and how we can go to heaven. That's what we mean by the saving Gospel message. God has clearly told us in His Word how we are saved.

Why will God allow us into heaven? Often when people are asked this question they answer that God will allow them to enter heaven because:

- They do good works.
- They try to be a good person.
- They're better or nicer than other people.
- God is love, or other answers of this type.

But, when we understand the Gospel we should answer something like, "God will allow me into heaven because of Jesus. He suffered and died for my sins and has prepared a place for me in heaven. There's nothing I can do obtain eternal life. I'm a sinner. Jesus has done it all!"

Salvation or eternal life is not a result of our good works. *"For by grace you have been saved through faith; and that not of yourselves, it is the gift of God; not as a result of works, so that no one may boast" (Ephesians 2:8-9).* It is God's free gift!

Remember the Gospel Is the Power of God for Salvation. An acronym that helps me remember what GRACE means is: God's Riches At Christ's Expense. Why not memorize this simple phrase?

The Bible always points us to Christ (John 5:39), and the Gospel is the "Good News" that Christ lived the life we couldn't live and did the work we couldn't do (1 Timothy 1:15). He lived a perfect life and suffered for our sins on the cross because we can't save ourselves. We are sinners! We must place our faith and trust in Him in order to obtain eternal life.

> An acronym that helps me remember what GRACE means is: God's Riches At Christ's Expense.

As Christians, we should be clear and precise when we speak about the Gospel. The Gospel shared by the apostles can be found in 1 Corinthians 15:1-7. Paul states, *"Now I would remind you, brothers, of the gospel I preached to you, which you received, in which you stand, and by which you are being saved, if you hold fast to the word I preached to you—unless you believed in vain" (1*

Corinthians 15:1-3, ESV). Paul states clearly that this Gospel saves us.

Paul goes on to define the Gospel. *"For I delivered to you as of first importance what I also received: that Christ died for our sins in accordance with the Scriptures, that He was buried, that He was raised on the third day in accordance with the Scriptures, and that He appeared to Cephas, then to the twelve. Then He appeared to more than five hundred brothers at one time, most of whom are still alive, though some have fallen asleep. Then He appeared to James, then to all the apostles. Last of all, as to one untimely born, He appeared to me"* (1 Corinthians 15:4-7, ESV).

This passage refers us back to "The Scriptures" or the Old Testament writing of the prophets. In Isaiah 53:4-12, we learn that Jesus was pierced for our transgressions, or sins. He was crushed for our iniquities; the chastening for our well-being fell upon Him, and by His scourging we are healed.

Romans 1:16 says, *"For I am not ashamed of the gospel, for it is the power of God for salvation to everyone who believes, to the Jew first and also to the Greek."*

1 Corinthians 1:18 says, *"For the word of the cross is foolishness to those who are perishing, but to us who are being saved it is the power of God."* The Gospel is God's power to save us!

One of the most familiar Bible passages is also one of the clearest in describing the Gospel, *"For God so loved the world that He gave His one and only Son, that whoever believes in Him [Jesus] shall not perish but have eternal life"* (John 3:16, TNIV).

Do you believe there is confusion about the Gospel? Why not consider a Gospel survey of your own? Ask several individuals, both within and outside of the church, the question, "What's the Gospel?" Be prepared for some interesting and challenging conversations!

Questions can be an excellent tool to open up conversations about spiritual topics. Jesus and the disciples used questions frequently. One example is recorded in Acts 8:26-40. Why not read it with your family this evening? Who told Philip to go? Whom did he approach? How did Philip begin the discussion? What happened next? What can you learn about witnessing from this brief encounter?

Some of you may be thinking, "I just don't feel equipped to share the

Gospel. Then be like Andrew, who, after meeting Jesus, brought his brother to meet Jesus (John 1:40-41). We can share the Gospel by bringing people to hear the message of the Gospel at our congregations. Invite them to special events, Bible studies, and worship services.

Here are some interesting statistics that originated in *Never on a Sunday: The Challenge of the Unchurched*, The Barna Research Group, 1990, p. 27. They asked the question: "What means of outreach communication would create a positive interest in your attending church?" Note the response and percentages:

A local church sponsored a concert or held a seminar on a topic of
personal interest 77%
A friend invited you to attend..71%
You received information in the mail 32%
Someone from a church in your community called you to tell you
about the church and invited you to attend........................35%
A pastor or church member visited your home and invited you to
attend 34%
You saw advertising on television or heard it on the radio 21%

How is your congregation reaching into the community? Why not encourage your congregation to organize a seminar or special event focused on reaching the unchurched within your community?

The harvest is plentiful. Remember when fruit is ripe you do not need to yank and pull on it. Seek to find those who are ripe for the harvest. Ask and answer questions. Listen to those going through trials and difficulties. Be willing to pray for them and offer your assistance. Show you care! Then, when God opens the door, share the saving Gospel message!

Engaging the Secular World in Spiritual Conversations

The hostess at the restaurant greeted me as I entered. The restaurant was empty so we continued to talk. She asked why I was at the conference center. I explained that I was a speaker at a Lutheran Parenting Convention being held in her city. As we began to get acquainted I asked about her and her family. She told me she had a 16-year-old daughter. I told her about my three grown children and that I was speaking at the conference on "Media and Its Impact on Today's Children." Soon she was telling me that she was having discipline problems with her daughter. She began to ask questions. "What does the Bible have to say about parenting? Does it say anything about discipline?" We visited for 10 minutes before another customer entered the restaurant. During those God-ordained minutes I learned she had come to the United States from Germany 12 years before, that her teenage daughter was causing her great concern, and that she hadn't attended church since before she left Germany. Before we ended the conversation, she asked me where she could find a church that would help her learn more about God and how to parent—God's way!

Conversations about spiritual issues frequently occur as I get acquainted with those I meet each day. How about you? Are you engaging people in conversations about life? And waiting for the Lord to open doors to talk about spiritual issues?

Did you know the unchurched population continues to skyrocket? Many of those who are unchurched (and even many within the church) don't know God's Word. For example: George Barna's Research has documented that 64 percent of those who are unchurched say that a good person can earn his or her way to heaven. And 44 percent of unchurched adults define God as an entity other than the perfect, all-powerful, all-knowing Creator of the universe. In the past three years, the unchurched adult population has risen. Now 40 percent of the Baby Boomers are unchurched and 38 percent of them are men. How will we reach these people for Christ? Learning to engage them in spiritual conversations is one way to begin.

> Are you engaging people in conversations about life? And waiting for the Lord to open doors to talk about spiritual issues?

How do we engage people in the secular world with a spiritual message? How can you and I learn to engage those we meet in conversations about spiritual issues? This was the topic of one Family Shield radio program. My guest was Rev. Steven Siegel, Director of United States Ministries of Lutheran Hour Ministries (www.lhm.org). He shared several stories of how he engages people in conversations about life. Frequently this leads to sharing a spiritual message. The following is one of his stories.

I travel a lot with my job. One evening I arrived late to pick up my reserved rental car and began a discussion with the young woman waiting on me. I was her last customer of the evening.

The discussion began as she asked my name. Rather than the normal reaction that I often get of 'Steven Segal – the actor', she said, "No I wasn't thinking of him, I was thinking of Bugsy Siegel."

I responded with laughter and said, "What does a young woman like yourself know about a 1920's gangster?" She explained that she had lived in Las Vegas for a while and had done a school report about him while she was in school.

We continued to get acquainted. Soon I asked her another question, "So, why are you working in Detroit?" She explained that she had been working in Las Vegas until recently, but had left when she had a great disappointment in her life. Soon she was telling me that she had been left at the altar on her wedding day. It had been a heartbreaking experience for her. She had taken the first job that came along just to get away. I extended my sympathy and listened to her as she shared her hurt, anger, and frustration. Then I shared a disappointment I had gone through. Being open and real about my life continued to open the door of opportunity.

Finally I asked, "So how are you doing dealing with these disappointments and challenges in your life—other than leaving Las Vegas?"

She responded, "Not very well."

Then I asked if I could share something that I thought might help her. I always ask permission to share information with those I meet. (Readers might be interested to know that Lutheran Hour Ministries offers a training seminar entitled, "Equipping to Share," which helps Christians learn how to do this effectively.) Seldom has anyone ever said "No" to this question. She said "Yes."

I told her that the God I knew was gracious, compassionate and loving, that He would walk with her through every challenge of life, and that He had a plan for her life. She listened attentively. Then she asked me several questions. Even though she was unchurched, she was interested in discussing spiritual issues! I ended our conversation by telling her I would pray for her. And I do!

Rev. Siegel said, "Kay, I could have closed down the discussion numerous times. I could have raised barriers by becoming angry that she had compared me to a 1920's gangster. I didn't. I just laughed when she made that comparison. I could have been judgmental or criticized her for selecting a fiancé who was an illegal immigrant or said something negative about her working in Las Vegas. Again, I didn't."

He concluded, "I begin each day by praying that the Lord will open a door for me to engage those I meet in spiritual conversations. He does! Doors fly open everywhere! I listen, show concern, ask questions, and am open about challenges I've faced in life. People like to talk about themselves. Just ask questions. Be real. And allow the Lord to open the doors."

Consider how you might engage those you meet each day in spiritual conversations. Pray that God will open doors of opportunity. Grow in God's grace. Study and grow in the knowledge of God's Word. Ask and respond to questions. Listen attentively. Show concern. Then 'go' through the door when God opens it.

"Go therefore and make disciples of all the nations, baptizing them in the name of the Father and the Son and the Holy Spirit, teaching them to observe all that I commanded you; and lo, I am with you always, even to the end of the age" (Matthew 28:19-20).

Evangelism and the Great Commission

Sharing the Gospel message of Jesus Christ is at the core of Family Shield Ministries' work in the ripe and plentiful harvest. Each year we respond to more than 7,000 people who contact us after hearing a radio program, discover the website, read one of our resources, or attend an educational seminar or workshop. About 10-15 percent of those we reach do not know Christ as their Savior and Lord. The Lord allows us many opportunities to minister to these people. Here is one example.

Brian, an active Mormon, discovered Family Shield's website at www.familyshieldministries.com. He e-mailed me and asked if the organization would promote the Book of Mormon on its website. I responded by explaining that we could not promote this book because the Church of Jesus Christ of Latter Day Saints is a cult. Of course, Brian disagreed. Brian and I continued to correspond through e-mail for several months. I eventually sent him one of the articles I'd written in 1995 that addressed "Mormon Teachings and Beliefs" and encouraged him to check out www.concernedchris-tians.org and www.josephlied.org. Both are Christian apologetic organizations. Soon after reviewing my articles and reviewing these websites he wrote one last time, "It's true I contacted you and asked you to help promote the Book of Mormon. I also asked you to stop saying the Mormon Church is a cult. You refuse to do this. I am warning you to stop fighting against the Lord's church! Your heart is hard, just as others have been over the years. You are a Pharisee. They, too, rejected the Prophets."

Although Brian is upset with me because I told him the Mormon Church is a cult and doesn't want to hear from me anymore, we continue to pray for him. Would you pray for Brian, too? Ask the Lord to reveal the truth about Christ to him and help him learn to discern truth from error.

We recognize this as an opportunity to share the Gospel of Christ with Brian. It's part of Family Shield's evangelism outreach work.

What is evangelism? Is evangelism a one-time encounter of sharing the Gospel with someone who does not know Christ, or is it more? The Body of Christ frequently refers to Matthew 28:18 as the "Great Commission." *"Go therefore and make disciples of all the nations, baptizing them in the name of the Father the Son and the Holy Spirit, and teaching them to ob-serve all that I commanded you."*

Please note that Matthew 28:18 does not say, "Share the message once and you're done." Rather it says to make them disciples, baptizing, and teaching them all that the Lord has commanded.

Here is a question to ponder. Is evangelism only about sharing the saving Gospel message with unbelievers, or is it more? What about the Great Commission? Isn't the Great Commission also about educating and equipping Christians in the Word so they can stand firm in the face of the evil one's attacks and learn to discern truth from error?

I believe evangelism is just one part of the Great Commission. The Great Commission is the entire process of helping an individual come to know Christ, grow up spiritually, become grounded in the Lord and His Word, and begin sharing with others that Jesus is the only means of salvation.

> Is evangelism a one-time encounter of sharing the Gospel with someone who does not know Christ, or is it more?

What do you think? What does God's Word say? What does Jesus say about this topic?

Did you know the word "evangelism" doesn't appear in the Bible? But, the word "evangelist" does. In Ephesians 4:11-12 we read about special gifts bestowed by the Holy Spirit, *"And He gave some as apostles, and some as prophets, and some as evangelists, and some as pastors and teachers, for the equipping of the saints for the work of service, to the building up of the body of Christ."* So, according to God's Word, an evangelist is a Christian who shares the Good News of Christ Jesus! Evangelists can be men or women. Evangelists work with pastors and teachers to equip Christians for the work of service in the Kingdom on earth.

Timothy was called an evangelist by the apostle Paul in 2 Timothy 4:5. He says, *"But you, be sober in all things, endure hardship, do the work of an evangelist, fulfill your ministry."*

In 2 Timothy 4:1-2, we find a list of some of the things an evangelist will do. Paul writes, *"I solemnly charge you in the presence of God and of Christ Jesus, who is to judge the living and the dead...preach the word; be ready in season and out of season; reprove, rebuke, exhort, with great patience and instruction."*

In 2 Timothy 3:15, we learn Timothy had known from childhood the sacred Scriptures which gave wisdom that leads to salvation through faith in Christ. This great eternal gift was shared with him by his grandmother, Lois, and his mother, Eunice.

How many of us have come to faith because of the loving care and spiritual impact of loved ones within our families? Would you agree with this statement? Evangelism is a family affair! Nurturing children as they grow into productive youth and from youth into Christian adults is certainly not a one-time affair. It is a work of service that often takes years of love, concern, and care.

An evangelist uses Scripture. 2 Timothy 3:16-17 (NIV) states, *"All Scripture is inspired by God and profitable for teaching, for reproof, for correction, for training in righteousness; so that the man of God may be adequate, equipped for every good work."*

How is your congregation or organization accomplishing its evangelism work? How are you equipping Christians to serve and witness? How are they partnering with others in the process?

> How is your congregation or organization accomplishing its evangelism work?

I am a member of The Lutheran Church—Missouri Synod. Here is what the LCMS is doing to encourage and equip its members to share Christ and help the Body of Christ accomplish The Great Commission. The Lutheran Church—Missouri Synod has begun a movement called *Ablaze!®—an initiative to ignite 100 million hearts with the Gospel.* This movement is based on Acts 14:27 (NIV) that says, *"They gathered the church together and reported all that God had done through them and how He opened the door of faith to the Gentiles."* At The Lutheran Church—Missouri Synod's July 2004 convention the delegates accepted the challenge from the LCMS World Mission and its North American and international church partners, to share the Good News of Jesus with 100 million people by 2017! This will be the 500 year anniversary of the Reformation. These contacts must be one-on-one Gospel presentations and include an opportunity for the person to respond to the Gospel message. The person may respond by receiving the message with gladness, rejecting it, or asking for additional information. To learn more about this exciting outreach movement, check out the website at www.lcmsworldmission.org/ablaze.

Working together, the Body of Christ can reach those who don't know Christ. *"But now righteousness from God, apart from law, has been made known, to which the Law and the Prophets testify. This righteousness from God comes through faith in Jesus Christ to all who believe. There is no difference, for all have sinned and fall short of the glory of God, and are justi-*

fied freely by his grace through the redemption that came by Christ Jesus. God presented him as a sacrifice of atonement, through faith in his blood" (Romans 3:21-25, NIV).

Witnessing Through the Internet

Have you ever witnessed to someone through the Internet? Many people do. I'm one of them, as is my son, Rev. Kevin T. Meyer, and my friend and co-worker in ministry, Dr. Jeff Schwehm. I'd like to encourage you to consider how you might do this with family members, friends, and strangers.

Dr. Schwehm is an ex-Jehovah's Witness. He frequently witnesses to Jehovah's Witnesses and their families. When he decided to leave the Watchtower Bible and Tract Society many years ago, a Christian man witnessed to him through the Internet. That Christian didn't just use words, he actually sent money to Jeff and his wife, Cathy. They desperately needed the funds to tide them over during this difficult time in their lives.

In my book, *Mission Field on Our Doorstep: Jehovah's Witnesses,* Jeff Schwehm shares stories of some of the people he reaches through the Internet. Jeff uses pseudonyms because most individuals associated with Jehovah's Witnesses must have their identities protected from retaliation by the leaders of the Watchtower Bible and Tract Society. Here are some of those stories:

> While discussing religious issues in an Internet chat room, I spoke with a Jehovah's Witness named "Emily" who wanted to discuss religion. During our discussion, it became apparent that "Emily" has serious doubts about her beliefs as a Jehovah's Witness. During the next few weeks, I was able to send her literature critical of some of the false doctrines of Jehovah's Witnesses. "Emily" and I correspond regularly via the Internet and the telephone on issues relating to the Jehovah's Witnesses. Please pray for "Emily."
>
> In another instance, I met a gentleman on the Internet named "David" who was thinking of being baptized as a Jehovah's Witness. However, there were still some issues he was dealing with that were preventing him from taking this last step toward joining

the organization. While speaking with him, I shared the scripture at John 5:24 and Ephesians 2:8-10, which clearly show that one is saved due to faith and not due to any works. In the next few weeks, "David" told me that he was no longer considering baptism by the JWs. He also told me he was interested in finding a church home that taught salvation was through Christ alone.

In another instance, I met an active Jehovah's Witness on the Internet whom we will call "Floyd." "Floyd" serves in his Kingdom Hall as a Deacon. During our conversation, "Floyd" shared with me his doubts about his beliefs as a Jehovah's Witness and we made arrangements to continue to discuss these doubts over the Internet.

But, how does Jeff find these people? I e-mailed Jeff last week and asked him what he does to reach interested people through the Internet. Here is what he shared:

> What I do is find a threaded discussion board that encourages discussion on Jehovah's Witnesses or Christian related issues. There are usually tons of them but a lot of times there are a couple of these boards that are really active.
>
> I just get on those message boards and make friends. Those individuals who want to learn more about the Christian faith usually wind up contacting me or going to my website for more information. I always make it a point to include a link to my website or to a good Christian article whenever I post a message on the board. Sometimes after individuals tell me that they would like to be a part of a Christian community I will encourage them, or help them, to find a Church to attend.
>
> I would say success occurs when you get an e-mail from someone who says, when discussing their new relationship with Jesus, "This is what I have been looking for my whole life!" I always get chills when that happens. It always amazes me that Jesus has allowed little insignificant me to help someone find Him.

My son, the Rev. Kevin T. Meyer, also witnesses through the Internet. Last year he witnessed to a man who lives in England. This man thought that Christians must be sinless after they come to faith in Christ. Kevin corrected this false teaching and continues to witness to him. Kevin also mailed him print resources and several audiocassettes from *Family Shield* radio programs that talked about the plan of salvation through Christ. Later he invited the man to listen to a *Family Shield* radio program that he hosted. (*Family Shield* is heard on three websites internationally: www.kfuo.org, www.wyll.net, and www.wluj.com.) And the man listened! Would you pray for this man? Pray that he would confess his sins, and commit his life to Christ.

Other things to think about as you consider witnessing through the Internet:

1. Pray and ask the Lord to lead you to witness in a God-pleasing manner. Allow Him to open the doors. Ask for His Wisdom as you write.
2. When witnessing through the Internet you will use the written word. It can be misunderstood. Be professional. Reread what you have written to make sure it says what you mean to say.
3. Recognize that witnessing this way will take time. Don't try to share everything at once.
4. It is important to share the Law and the Gospel. People need to understand why they need a Savior and then to hear "Good News."
5. You may sometimes need to correct false teachings. Do your research, and back up what you say with Scripture.
6. Know the Word of God. Become prepared by attending Bible studies, attending witnessing training classes, and be in the Word.
7. Don't continue to write to people that do not respond. Make sure the person you are writing is interested in continuing the Internet conversation.

I pray that something in this section will help you consider how you might witness through the Internet.

"Do not let your hearts be troubled. Trust in God; trust also in me. In My Father's house are many rooms; if it were not so, I would have told you. I am going there to prepare a place for you. And if I go and prepare

a place for you, I will come back and take you to be with me that you also may be where I am" (John 14:1-3, NIV).

"I am the way and the truth and the life. No one comes to the Father except through me. If you really knew me, you would know my Father as well" (John 14:6-7, NIV).

Making the Most of Brief Encounters

You're flying home after a business trip and begin a conversation with the woman sitting next to you. She tells you her father is dying of cancer. How could you use this brief encounter to share words of encouragement and hope? Your faith in Christ? Brief encounters like this occur every day.

The following is written to help you: 1) See how Jesus, the apostles, and disciples used brief encounters; 2) Recognize God-given opportunities to share the Gospel through brief encounters; 3) Equip yourself to share God's love when a brief encounter occurs; and 4) Grow in the grace and knowledge of our Lord Jesus Christ and the Word of God.

How did Jesus, the apostles, and disciples use brief encounters to share their faith? Jesus had brief encounters with the women who touched him (Mark 5:25-34); the woman at the well (John 4:7-29); and the thief on the

cross (Luke 23:32, 39-43). Can you think of other brief encounters the Lord had?

The apostles and disciples also had many brief encounters. Paul had a brief encounter with Stephen (Acts 7:58-60); and with the jailer (Acts 16:25-34). Priscilla and Aquila had a brief encounter with Apollos (Acts 18:24-28). Can you think of other brief encounters they had?

I've had hundreds of brief encounters over the years. Here are a few examples.

While traveling: I frequently strike up conversations with those near me when I travel. I almost always have an opportunity to share my faith in Christ. Sometimes it's to Christians who are going through trials and struggles. At other times I have opportunity to witness to those who are unchurched, fallen away from the faith, Christians who are trusting in their works rather than Christ, or those involved in a false religion or cult.

- I remember an interesting conversation with a Muslim as I traveled to Canada a few years ago. Rather than telling him his religion was wrong, I began asking him questions about what Muslims believed and then explained what I believed as a Christian. It wasn't long before he was asking me questions about the Christian faith!

> I frequently strike up conversations with those near me when I travel. I almost always have an opportunity to share my faith in Christ.

- I was flying home from a business trip and began a conversation with a young mother sitting next to me. She told me she was returning home after seeing her father who recently suffered a heart attack. As we talked I learned she did not attend church. When she found out I worked for a Christian ministry she asked, "Do you really believe people go to heaven when they die?" It was an interesting conversation.

At work and in the community: Opportunities to share my faith and witness arise naturally as I interact with people in the community and through the ministry.

- I was an exhibitor at a national convention and got into a conversation with a woman who had recently lost her 80-year old mother. She shared, "My mother was my best friend. I miss her so much." I listened and showed concern. Then I asked if I could pray with her. We prayed together in the middle of the busy convention center. I asked the Lord to help her through this difficult time. Later I sent her a tape of a program we had produced on "The Grieving Process."
- I met with a vendor about the production of a new resource. Getting acquainted, I asked him about his family and then later where he and his family fellowship. He told me they don't attend church, but that he used to be Catholic. This led to a short, fruitful discussion about the Lord and the forgiveness He offers every day. I en-

couraged him not to forsake assembling of ourselves together and to be a model for his family. I also told him we could recommend a few congregations near his home.

- Family Shield receives thousands of calls, e-mails, and letters each year at our office and through the Response Center from individuals and family members who tune in to our radio program or read about the ministry. Some are Christians, many are not. We try to assist them with specific needs and connect them to individuals, organizations, or products that can assist them. Then, as the Lord leads, we share the Gospel, God's Word, and encourage them to become active in a local congregation.

What about you? Have you had brief encounters? Prayerfully consider how you can more effectively share your faith when brief encounters occur. Ask God to forgive you if you've blown opportunities in the past. Ask Him to help you do a better job next time, and grant you wisdom to share His love with others in the future.

If you are like me, you've probably blown many brief encounters. You and I are not alone. So did the apostle Peter. Read the following story and think about how Peter blew this opportunity to share his faith (Matthew 26:69-75).

"Now Peter was sitting outside in the court-yard, and a servant-girl came to him and said, 'You too were with Jesus the Galilean.' But he denied it before them all, saying, 'I do not know what you are talking about.' When he had gone out to the gateway, another servant-girl saw him and said to those who were there, 'This man was with Jesus of Nazareth.' And again he denied it with an oath, 'I do not know the man.' A little later the bystanders came up and said to Peter, 'Surely you too are one of them; for even the way you talk gives you away.' Then he began to curse and swear. 'I do not know the man!'" (Matthew 26:69-72).

Why not ask God to help you more effectively share your faith the next time He opens a door?

Remember, Jesus said, "Follow me and I will make you fishers of men." Watch for those brief encounters. Ask questions. Answer questions. Then rely upon the Holy Spirit to guide and direct you. He will give you the words in the hour you need them.

Meeting the Needs of the Body, Mind, and Spirit

"My wife and I live in a motel in Chicago with our two small children," wrote Michael. "We're homeless. We have no car, no savings, no checking, and no credit. I have a job, but no medical insurance. I am 35 years old and am not addicted to drugs or alcohol. We are homeless because I made an error in judgment. I accepted a job in another state. The company I worked for in Chicago was bought out. My boss promised us that all the moving expenses would be covered if I took the new job in Colorado. It was a little more money than I'd been making. Rent was more reasonable than Chicago. After moving, they discovered my boss had been embezzling funds. He disappeared. Then I learned the company had not agreed to pay our moving expenses. We couldn't afford to pay the moving company either. We lost all our furniture, clothes, photos, and vital records. It took months, but we were finally able to move back to Chicago. I take public transportation to and from work so I'm gone from 7:30 a.m. until 7:30 p.m. We barely survive week to week. The motel costs $600 a month. Can you help? We've been praying and praying to God for help. I found your website and thought maybe your organization could assist us."

Family Shield received this e-mail in March of 2003. We receive thousands of calls, letters, and e-mails each year from individuals with a wide range of needs. Some are physical or mental needs, others are spiritual. It took fervent prayer, almost two months, many phone calls, letters, and e-mails, but we were finally able to partner with Lutheran Church Charities in the Chicago area and help obtain food, medical assistance, temporary housing, and reliable transportation for this couple and their two small children. We praise God for allowing us to be part of His Kingdom Work. We continue to pray for Michael, Serrina, and their two boys. Sometimes, the body of Christ must offer help with physical needs before it can effectively share the Gospel. It is often during times of crisis that individuals cry out to the Lord for help. God uses times of crisis to

> God uses times of crisis to draw us closer to Him!

draw us closer to Him!

Congregations and Christian non-profit ministries must meet the needs of the body, mind, and spirit! Jesus didn't just tell people about God's love and forgiveness. He also met physical needs. Jesus and His disciples fed the hungry. Jesus also healed the sick, the blind, and the crippled. And He told those He assisted about the Kingdom of God.

Today many congregations divide various aspects of ministry among different boards or committees. They may include the Board of Evangelism, the Board of Education, the Board of Human Care, the Board of Elders, and the Board of Social Ministry. This separation of duties is logical, but sometimes causes us to forget that we must work together.

Let me share two examples of how my congregation worked together to meet the needs of families within our community. I was chairman of the Board of Evangelism. As chairman, one of my responsibilities was to attend a monthly council meeting. It was there that I learned the Board for Social Ministry was offering financial assistance to individuals and families who lived in our community. Sometimes they helped people in the community

 who were unemployed with financial support to help pay their rent or utilities. At other times they delivered food and other needed supplies. I asked if these families were invited to our worship services. I was told, "No." We recognized that some of these families that were helped had no relationship with Christ. We began talking about how the two boards and their volunteers could work cooperatively. I was told that those on the Board for Social Ministry were often people who felt uncomfortable sharing their faith. They liked to show their faith through actions!

I knew our outreach committee could help. I asked the Board for Social Ministry to give the Board of Evangelism the names, addresses, and telephone numbers of the individuals they assisted on a monthly basis. The outreach committee, who were trained and equipped to share their faith, began visiting the homes of those who had been assisted through the Board for Social Ministry. We decided brief doorstep visits would be the best approach. They rang the doorbell and then explained who they were and what church they were associated with. They extended an invitation to visit the church and to send their children to Sunday school. They gave them a brochure about the church and tracts that shared the Gospel. Families were warm and friendly. Members were often invited inside to talk further. God opened many doors for further discussion about the Christian faith. Those we visited knew that our congregation assisted them when they needed help. They knew the members of this congregation cared about them and their family.

Here is a second example of how we worked together. Our church had a Christian school. I learned that no one was responsible for contacting unchurched parents with children in school to invite them to the worship and Bible studies. The Board of Evangelism again requested the names, addresses, and telephone numbers of families with children in the school who did not attend our congregation. This time the committee decided that making a telephone call first would work best. Again, the results were positive. Many families began attending the worship services and Bible studies due to these calls and visits.

Please note that communication and cooperation is critical! God does not expect us to do the work alone!

Are your church's committees and boards communicating effectively? Does one hand know what the other hand is doing? How about your Christian non-profit ministry? Are you working together? Why not consider how you can work together in sharing God's love with those in need?

"Jesus was going though all the cities and villages, teaching in their synagogues and proclaiming the gospel of the kingdom, and healing every kind of disease and every kind of sickness. Seeing the people, He felt compassion for them, because they were distressed and dispirited like sheep without a shepherd. Then He said to His disciples, 'The harvest is plentiful, but the workers are few. Therefore beseech the Lord of the harvest to send out workers into His harvest'" (Matthew 9:35-38).

Proclaim the Law—Then Share the Gospel

Recently, while teaching a Bible study at a home for women who have chosen life, a new, unchurched resident asked a question after a reference was made to the Ten Commandments. She asked, "Does one of those Ten Commandments say we shouldn't curse? The house parents and several residents continue to tell me not to curse, but I never knew why." I explained that one of the commandments does say, "Do not take the name of the Lord in vain." We discussed what this commandment means. Then I told her we would review the Ten Commandments the following week.

Often, when we try to witness to those who do not know Christ, we forget that the Law must be proclaimed so they understand why they need a Savior. It does little good to proclaim the Gospel to those who do not think they are sinners in need of forgiveness. Proclaim the Law first! Then share the Gospel!

Can you find the Ten Commandments in your Bible? Can you quote all Ten Commandments from memory? If not, why not strive to memorize one each week for the next 10 weeks? You can find them in Exodus. *"And God spoke all these words: I am the Lord your God, who brought you out of Egypt, out of the land of slavery. You shall have no other gods before me. You shall not make for yourself an idol in the form of anything in heaven above or on the earth beneath or in the waters below. You shall not bow down to them or worship them; for I, the* LORD *your God, am a jealous God, punishing the children for the sin of the fathers to the third and fourth generation of those who hate me, but showing love to a thousand generations, of those who love me and keep my commandments. You shall not misuse the name of the* LORD *your God, for the* LORD *will not hold anyone guiltless who misuses His name. Remember the Sabbath day by keeping it holy. Six days you shall labor and do all your work, but the seventh day is a Sabbath to the* LORD *your God. On it you shall not do any work, neither you, nor your son or daughter, nor your manservant or maidservant, nor your animals, nor the alien within your gates. For in six days the* LORD *made the heavens and the earth, the sea, and all that is in them, but he rested on the seventh day. Therefore the* LORD *blessed the Sabbath day and made it holy. Honor your father and your mother, so that you may live long in the land the* LORD *your God is giving you. You shall not murder. You shall not commit adultery. You shall not steal. You shall not give false testimony against your neighbor. You shall not covet your neighbor's house. You shall not covet your neighbor's wife, or his manservant or maidservant, his ox or donkey, or anything that belongs to your* neighbor" (Exodus 20:1-17).

The Ten Commandments convict us of our sin and the need of forgiveness from God. They are also a guide for living. But from Scripture we learn we cannot keep the Ten Commandments perfectly because we are sinners, even as Christians.

Christ came to save sinners (1 Timothy 1:15). He is the only perfect, sinless person that ever lived! James 2:10 (NIV) tells us when we break one commandment, we've broken them all. It reads, *"For whoever keeps the whole law and yet stumbles at just one point is guilty of breaking all of it."* That's why Christians continue to confess their sins to God and ask for His forgiveness.

Once you've shared the Law, the Gospel message is "Good News!" 1 Corinthians 15:1-7 (NIV) states, *"Now, brothers, I want to remind you of the gospel I preached to you, which you received and on which you have taken your stand. By this gospel you are saved, if you hold firmly to the word I preached to you. Otherwise, you have believed in vain. For what I received I passed on to you as of first importance: that Christ died for our sins according to the Scriptures, that he was buried, that he was raised on the third day according to the Scriptures, and that he appeared to Peter, and then to the Twelve. After that, he appeared to more than five hundred of the brothers at the same time, most of whom are still living, though some have fallen asleep. Then he appeared to James, then to all the apostles, and last of all he appeared to me [Paul] also, as to one abnormally born."*

For additional information about this topic, order a copy of the *Family Shield* radio program entitled, "Law and Gospel," which features Dr. James Kalthoff, the former president of the LCMS Missouri District.

May I encourage you to proclaim the Law first, then share the Gospel with those who do not know Christ?

"For if, when we were God's enemies, we were reconciled to him through the death of his Son, how much more, having been reconciled, shall we be saved through his life! Not only is this so, but we also rejoice in God through our Lord Jesus Christ, through whom we have now received reconciliation" (Romans 5:10-11, NIV).

Grow Up!

Why don't you grow up?! Have you ever said something like this to someone who was acting childish or silly? Has anyone ever said this to you? We all grow physically, but not all Christians grow spiritually. God desires that we "grow up in Him!"

"And He gave some as apostles, and some as prophets, and some as evangelists, and some as pastors and teachers, for the equipping of the saints for the work of service, to the building up of the body of Christ; until we all attain to the unity of the faith, and of the knowledge of the Son of God, to a mature man, to the measure of the stature which belongs to the fullness of Christ. As a result, we are no longer to be children, tossed here and there by waves, and carried about by every wind of doctrine, by the trickery of men, by craftiness in deceitful scheming; but speaking the truth in love, we are to grow up in all aspects into Him, who is the head, even Christ, from whom the whole body, being fitted and held together by what every joint supplies, according to the proper working of each individual part, causes the growth of the body for the building up of itself in love" (Ephesians 4:11-16).

The above verses warn that if we do not grow spiritually, we are in danger of being blown about by every wind of doctrine. In other words, we might be deceived into believing false teachings and false prophets.

Did you know that God's Word says some people preach another Jesus and a different gospel? *"If one comes and preaches another Jesus whom we have not preached, or you receive a different spirit which you have not received, or a different gospel which you have not accepted, you bear this beautifully (2 Corinthians 11:4).* Have you ever met someone who preaches another Jesus or a different gospel? Were you able to defend your faith and effectively explain what the Bible really teaches about Christ and the Gospel to them?

Did you know that the apostle Paul was shocked that some Christians deserted the one who called them by the grace of Christ and had turned to a different gospel? Hear what Paul writes. *"I am astonished that you are so quickly deserting the one who called you by the grace of Christ and are turning to a different gospel—which is really no gospel at all. Evidently some people are throwing you into confusion and are trying to pervert the gospel of Christ. But* even if we or an angel from heaven should preach a gospel other than the one we preached to you, let him be eternally condemned!" (Galatians 1:6, NIV).

What was the Gospel that Paul preached? "Now I make known to you, brethren, the gospel which I preached to you, which also you received, in which also you stand, by which also you are saved, if you hold fast the word which I preached to you, unless you believed in vain. For I delivered to you as of first importance which I also received, that Christ died for our sins according to the Scriptures, and that He was buried, and that He was raised on the third day according to the Scriptures, and that He appeared to Cephas, then to the twelve. After that He appeared to more than 500 brethren at one time, most of whom remain until now, but some have fallen asleep; then He appeared to James, then to all the apostles; and last of all, as to one untimely born, He appeared to me also" (1 Corinthians 15:1-8).

As we grow spiritually we will begin to understand that Jesus Christ is true God and true man. "In the beginning was the Word, and the Word was with God, and the Word was God" (John 1:1). "See to it that no one takes you captive through philosophy and empty deception, according to the traditions of men, according to the elementary principles of the world, rather than according to Christ. For in Him all the fullness of Deity dwells in bodily form, and in Him you have been made complete, and He is the head over all rule and authority" (Colossians 2:8-10).

As we grow we will be able to share the Gospel in a more effective way with those who do not know Him as their Savior and Lord. We will understand that although we have forgiveness, we cannot live a perfect life. We are still sinners and are in need of forgiveness. "If we say that we have no sin, we are deceiving ourselves, and the truth is not in us. If we confess our sins, He is faithful and righteous to forgive us our sins and to cleanse us from all unrighteousness. If we say that we have not sinned, we make Him a liar, and His word is not in us" (1 John 1:8-10). Christ came to live the perfect life we are unable to live (see Matthew 5:48).

As we grow spiritually we will more effectively defend our faith and live our faith in the home, in the community, and in the workplace. And when we fail, which we will, we know we have a loving and forgiving Savior! So what are you waiting for? Grow up!

Motivating Members and Organizing Congregations for Outreach

Jeff was raised in a non-Christian home that was not kind to Christians. For years he argued with Christians he met telling them they were crazy to believe in God. Then he met a man who believed in prayer. Dick began praying for Jeff and asked his small prayer group to pray for him also. He prayed for many years. He also witnessed to Jeff when opportunities arose in a kind and loving way. Because they were friends Jeff listened. It took over five years, but today Jeff is a committed Christian. He is active in his congregation and loves to tell others about Christ. He now prays for his extended family.

PREPARING MEMBERS TO WITNESS

- **Begin with Prayer.** Prayer is the most important aspect involved in motivating congregational members to be interested in witnessing. Motivate members to be organized for outreach by helping them see the importance of prayer. Encourage them to pray for unchurched relatives, friends, and co-workers. Pray together, asking for God's guidance and direction concerning how your congregation and its members can become motivated and organized for outreach.

- **Encourage members to be in the Word.** Recognize that busy schedules may not make it possible for members to attend a Sunday morning Bible study. Encourage members to read Portals of Prayer and other devotional material. Recommend good Christian books, Bible studies, audiocassettes, websites, DVDs, and videos in your newsletter. Place a daily devotion or Bible study on the Internet. Share suggestions for witnessing in your monthly newsletter. Encourage members to listen to Christian radio and to read the Bible each day.

- **Offer options in your Bible study program.** Don't just have a Bible class on Sunday mornings. Have an early morning weekday Bible study for working members, begin a home Bible study program, and offer Bible studies on weekdays and/or Saturdays.

- **Use the spiritual gifts the Lord has given your members.** Use those who are gifted in teaching and witnessing, but don't exclude anyone. Find a place for any willing worker. Those with the gift of service, hospitality, or administration can serve food after an outreach event, baby-sit for those who go out on evangelism calls, assist with coordination details and do record-keeping.

- **Pastors, preach about witnessing!** I am so thankful that my pastor not only shared the Law and Gospel from the pulpit, but also encouraged us to share our faith with others. Don't underestimate the importance of the words you share on Sunday mornings from the pulpit. God's Word does not return void. Members will hear and, led by the Spirit, respond.

- **Equip members to share their faith.** Training is critical! Remember that members who are equipped to share their faith will have hundreds of opportunities to witness in the home, at work, and in their community. Recognize that those opportunities might not bring new members to your congregation. It might not get members involved in a formal outreach program of the congregation. But their witness can bring people to the foot of the cross!

- **Organize outreach efforts.** Consider various ways your congregation might organize your outreach efforts. Some congregations believe it is essential to have a Board of Evangelism, charged with equipping members to grow and witness. Other congregations prefer not to have such a board. Since each congregation is unique, how you organize for outreach may be different from other congregations.

- **Work cooperatively with other boards and committees.** Involve various boards and organizational groups within your congregation in witnessing. If your congregation has 12 boards, organizations and groups, each month a different board, organization or group could be assigned to make telephone calls or personal visits to visitors. While making visits they extend an invitation to attend church and Bible class. They then fill out a simple form and return it to the church so records are kept. Or, plan a special friendship event and assign different boards and committees specific responsibilities.

- **Set goals and objectives**. All congregations should develop goals and objectives concerning outreach. Make them realistic and attainable.

DEVELOPING LEVELS OF PARTICIPATION

It helps to have your congregation offer different levels (or styles) of witnessing opportunities for members. Level one provides non-threatening ways to get involved in sharing Christ. Those who become involved in level one may not feel equipped to share the Gospel, but want to share their faith. These members can be like Andrew, who after meeting Jesus, brought his brother to meet Jesus (John 1:40-41). They can share the Gospel by bringing people to hear the Law and Gospel being proclaimed at worship services. They can share print resources and invite those who don't know Christ to special events at your congregation.

Level One
- **Tract Ministry**. Keep the tract racks filled and appropriate to the time of year, and take Christian tracts to local hospitals, doctors offices, college campuses and public libraries. (It's best to ask permission to leave them in most secular locations.) The person in charge of this ministry can also be responsible for ordering tracts. Encourage members to leave tracts at restaurants with their tips and include them when paying bills and sending cards. Tracts are available from Concordia Publishing House, 3558 S. Jefferson, St. Louis, MO 63118, (314) 268-1000.
- **Tape Ministry**. Many churches offer audiocassettes of sermons to members. This ministry can be expanded to reach out into the community. Tell your members that audiocassettes are also available for their churched and unchurched friends. You might even advertise this service in secular newspapers.
- **Servant Outreach Evangelism**. "We couldn't wait to tell the shoppers about the greatest gift of all...Jesus, the Savior of the World!"
  Several years ago, members of St. Mark's Lutheran Church in Eureka, Missouri, used the Saturday before Christmas to witness to their community in a unique way. The local Wal-Mart store gave

them permission to have a gift-wrapping table in the storefront. As shoppers entered the store they were handed a tract that said: "Two free gifts for you." The first message was simple: "Our greatest Christmas gift is from God. He sent His only Son, Jesus Christ, who grants us forgiveness of sins and eternal life. And, His gift is free! It's for you!"

The second message was that shoppers could have one Christmas gift wrapped free as they left the store. While shoppers waited to have their gifts wrapped, they were a captive audience for church volunteers who were wrapping the presents. Many shoppers tried to give a donation. That just made the "free gift" message concerning Jesus even more meaningful to share! Other congregations can use this type of servant event. Be creative. Use ideas like free car washes or Easter egg hunts with a Christian message. Teenagers can rake leaves for older residents within their community, Bible study groups can deliver cookies to area nursing homes, etc.

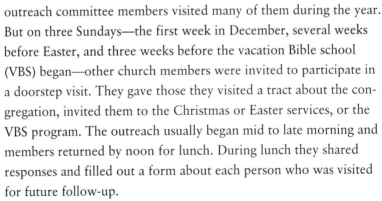

- **Sunday morning newcomer outreach.** Ascension Lutheran Church, St. Louis, had three Sundays each year when they coordinated a Sunday morning newcomer outreach. From the Council of Lutheran Churches they received names and addresses of individuals who moved into their community. The outreach committee members visited many of them during the year. But on three Sundays—the first week in December, several weeks before Easter, and three weeks before the vacation Bible school (VBS) began—other church members were invited to participate in a doorstep visit. They gave those they visited a tract about the congregation, invited them to the Christmas or Easter services, or the VBS program. The outreach usually began mid to late morning and members returned by noon for lunch. During lunch they shared responses and filled out a form about each person who was visited for future follow-up.

- **Delivering bread to visitors.** When visiting, it helps to have something to give to them when you arrive on their doorstep. Many congregations deliver small loaves of bread. Even if the visitor is not home, the gift can be left along with one tract about the congregation and one tract that shares the plan of salvation.

Level Two

- **Fair Booth Ministry.** Thousands of Christian groups participate in sharing their faith by handing out literature with a Christ-centered message at state and local fairs. To learn more about resources available, write Lutheran Hour Ministries, Fair Booth Ministry, 660 Mason Ridge Center Drive, St. Louis, MO 63141.
- **Plan a special event, seminar, or concert.** While I was chairman of Ascension Lutheran Church's Evangelism Board, we worked with other boards, committees, and organizations within the congregation to plan numerous special events that encouraged members to bring an unchurched friend or relative. Those on the planning committee used their gifts of administration and leadership to help make the events a powerful tool for reaching out with the Gospel.

One of our most exciting and family-oriented events was the International Friendship Festival. Below is an excerpt from an article that was published about this event:

A few years ago, when Ascension Lutheran Church in St. Louis held an "evangelism Sunday" event, just seven members brought friends to the service. The next year, the congregation's evangelism board did things a little differently.

Its "International Friendship Festival," held at the church's grade school, gave visitors a taste of life in Nigeria and Brazil. In the process, it gave them a small dose of Christianity, too.

In one classroom—transformed overnight into a Brazilian jungle complete with lush tropical vegetation, exotic stuffed animals and a paper Amazon River—children sat cross-legged on the floor, listening to Christian stories from another culture. Three other classrooms in the "Children's Center" offered craft activities, games and a display of foreign clothing and masks.

In the gym, visitors could choose from a myriad of activities:

learning to speak a Bible verse in Portuguese or an African dialect, watching an international fashion show, meeting missionaries and nationals from Nigeria and Brazil, watching videos on the two spotlighted countries, singing and dancing a la Africa, sampling Brazilian coffee or African bean cakes, and viewing numerous displays and posters on the two countries.

Like any mission-centered fair, Gospel messages were prevalent throughout the festival. But this was more than your typical mission fair. Although it involved the congregation's mission board, as well as the parish school and women's guild, the event was the brainstorm of the evangelism board. As a result, follow-up on unchurched visitors played a big part in the production. And the festival likely made a more positive impact on non-Christian visitors than would any "evangelism Sunday" event.

- **Prayer Breakfast.** Ascension Lutheran Church also coordinated a monthly prayer breakfast. The goal was to encourage members to invite an unchurched friend. Each prayer breakfast included cereal, donuts, juice, coffee, fellowship, and a speaker who shared how he had come to faith in Christ or how the Lord had been working in his life. The program always included the Gospel message and time for prayer.
- **Support Groups.** Families deal with so many issues today. Another way some congregations reach out into the community is to offer support groups for family members and friends. They open the doors of their congregation to those in the community. There are support groups for recovering alcoholics, those who have been on drugs, family members and friends of homosexuals, family members and friends of Jehovah's Witnesses—the list goes on. How could your congregation reach out through a support group? What types of support groups might be appropriate for your congregation? Most importantly, how will you share the Gospel with those who attend?
- **Public Relations.** Recognize that there is a close relationship between public relations and effective outreach. Don't forget to use media opportunities to reach the community. No matter what type

of outreach ministry your congregation chooses, congregational leaders need to learn how to use media tools that are available to reach beyond the church walls. How can you use public service announcements to share information with the community about your congregation? How can you write news releases that will get published? Do you have members in your congregation who are used to writing news releases and public service announcements? Involve them in your outreach efforts.

Level Three

Level three may involve confrontational evangelism. Those involved in this type of evangelism are usually equipped not only to model their faith, but also verbalize their faith. Many individuals are reluctant to become involved in this style of outreach because they feel ill-equipped to share their faith, are afraid someone will ask them a question they cannot answer, or because they do not have the gift of evangelism and/or teaching. Those who are interested in this style of outreach are usually active in Bible study and are spiritually mature.

To be effective, these people need good interpersonal communication skills. They also need to know and use available resources. A number of excellent resources are listed below. Additional resources include Christian and secular organizations and agencies; and other church members or individuals with knowledge and ability. When you are aware of resources, you can refer and connect those in need to them.

- **Dialog Evangelism and Dialog Evangelism II.** The calling team-training material has been developed by the LCMS.
- **Evangelism Explosion.** This program, developed by James D. Kennedy, is used by thousands of congregations. It includes both training and on-the-job training in visiting people within their homes.
- **Cult Evangelism.** The Family Shield Cult Outreach Ministry, which I have been involved in since 1981, grew out of my involvement in witnessing to Jehovah's Witnesses and their family mem-

bers and friends. We witness to individuals involved in the Watchtower Society, offer training to Christians, and connect families and friends to Christian resources that can assist them. Hundreds of other organizations specialize in witnessing to cults and/or the occult. For a list of apologetic organizations, write: Family Shield, P. O. Box 230015, St. Louis, MO 63123.

- **Commission on Organizations.** The Lutheran Church—Missouri Synod Commission on Organizations also shares information with those who have questions about cults and the occult. For information write: Dr. Jerald Joersz, The LCMS Commission on Organizations, 1333 S. Kirkwood Rd., St. Louis, MO 63122.

- **Jews for Jesus and Apple of His Eye Mission Society.** These organizations specialize in witnessing to Jews who do not believe in Christ. They witness directly to Jewish people, offer training, and distribute tracts.

Remember the Gospel is the Power of God for Salvation. An acronym for GRACE is God's Riches at Christ's Expense. Romans 1:16 says, *"For I am not ashamed of the gospel, for it is the power of God for salvation to everyone who believes, to the Jew first and also to the Greek."* 1 Corinthians 1:18 says, *"For the word of the cross is foolishness to those who are perishing, but to us who are being saved it is the power of God."* The Gospel is God's power to save us!

Christ came for all people! His forgiveness is for everyone! Pray, be in the Word, use various styles of outreach, use available resources, and rely upon the Holy Spirit to guide and direct your congregation's efforts. Then learn from the Lord Himself how to become "fishers of men."

Reaching Families Through Christian Schools

Thousands of parents and grandparents, many who do not know Christ, walk into Christian schools each year. They enroll their children for a variety of reasons. Some are fearful of the public school system, others believe "a little religion is good for children," or they heard from a neighbor that the school "offers a quality education." Whatever the reason, church leaders and school administrators must recognize that schools can reach families for Christ.

You are probably aware that the United States is a mission field. So are Christian schools! There are over 208 million adults living in the United States. George Barna (www.barna.org) estimates there are 125 million unchurched adults. This number includes 29 million who claim no religion, plus those who say they are Christians but never go to church. In addition there are 2.8 million who are of the Jewish faith, 1.3 million Jehovah's Witnesses, 2.7 million Mormons, 1.1 million Muslims, and 1.1 million Buddhists. How can we reach them? One avenue is through your Christian school.

The following is the story of one family who came to know Christ because they enrolled their two children in a Christian school.

Stephen, a recovering alcoholic, had come to know "a god" he referred to as "the Higher Power" prior to enrolling his two children in the school, but he admits he did not know Jesus Christ.

Stephen's young daughter was confined to a wheelchair. He wanted her to attend "a regular school." As he drove by a school near their home, he noticed there were no steps. He went home and announced to his wife, "I've found the school the children can attend. Brenda won't have trouble getting in and out of that school in her wheelchair!" Only after they'd driven over to see the school did they discover it was a Christian school.

> Now I understand that religion isn't a bunch of rules and regulations, but a personal relationship with Jesus Christ!

After enrolling the two children, he and his wife noticed the loving care of the staff. They attended parent teacher meetings and other school functions. Soon they met other parents who attended the congregation that sponsored the school.

A pastor's class was advertised in the school newspaper. Their son's teacher called and invited them to attend. At first Stephen resisted, but finally he and his wife agreed to attend the weekly class.

Stephen later stated, "I had been turned off by 'organized religion' when I was young. When I began those classes, all religion was to me was a bunch of rules and regulations. But during the class I learned of God's love and of His forgiveness! I learned God sent His only Son, Jesus Christ, into the world to save sinners. I was one of those sinners. Now I understand that religion isn't a bunch of rules and regulations, but a personal relationship with Jesus Christ! Jesus suffered and died for me! I'm so glad we decided to put our children in this school. That decision changed my life eternally!

What can your school do to reach family members who don't know Christ? The following are some suggestions to consider.

- **Be aware that many parents who place their children within Christian schools don't know Christ as their Savior and Lord.** Make an effort to reach them during the short time they are a part of the school family. Invite them to church, Sunday school, vacation Bible school, Bible classes and special events.
- **Work together.** To be most effective takes cooperation, planning, prayer, and time on the part of the educators, administrators, and congregational leaders.
- **Demonstrate faith through action and words.** Share how knowing Christ has gotten you through trials or how God has answered your prayers. Let the parents know you care about their needs.
- **Use every opportunity to share Christ.** Many teachers make home visits. Begin home visits with a prayer and/or devotion. Ask the parents if they have any needs or concerns that you can include in your prayers. Many times knowing needs becomes the open door at a later date for sharing the Gospel.
- **Encourage family devotions.** Share ideas through your newsletter concerning how to present family devotions.
- **Encourage parents to help children with memory verses.** Teachers should make assigned verses focus on God's love in Christ. Keep them simple. Share ways parents can work with the children.
- **Pray** (Matthew 7:7; 18:19, 20).
  - Teach children to pray. They will share their faith with their parents.

- Form a prayer group of co-workers and parents to meet weekly to pray for the needs of your school and families.
- Encourage parents to begin a classroom prayer chain.
- Share prayer requests with your pastor and church staff to include in worship and prayer meetings.
- Encourage mothers to become involved in *Moms in Touch*, and other prayer groups.

- **Involve church staff and leaders**
  - Share names of unchurched families within your school with your pastor and/or chairman of the Board of Evangelism.
  - Become acquainted with family resources. If a parent is unemployed, share community and congregational resources. Does your social ministry offer help and financial assistance to families in need? What other resources are available within your community? In the church?

- **Involve Parent and Teacher Groups**
  - Review the constitution and bylaws. Establish annual goals that include spiritual growth.
  - Open each meeting with a devotion that shares the Savior's love and forgiveness.
  - Include children in at least one event each year. When children are involved, their parents usually are, too.
  - Consider offering an annual training workshop on parenting. Offer Christ-centered topics, but also address subjects that may attract the parents who do not attend church. Popular topics include: "Discipline in the Home"; "Coping with Difficult People"; "Dealing with Anger"; "Building Healthy Self-Esteem in Our Children"; "Stress Management and Time Management." Don't forget to offer baby-sitting.
  - Fellowship opportunities are important. Include mixers during meetings so parents get to know each other. Organize a potluck dinner. Consider cooperating with other church groups. This offers the opportunity for unchurched parents to meet others from your congregation in a setting where they don't feel threatened.

- Plan one or more fun, interesting family events that involve both the school and congregational members. Suggestions include an international friendship festival, Reformation Festival, Family Fun or Game Night, and/or a Halloween alternative.

Finally, don't forget to equip your teachers so they can share Christ with the children and parents. And, make the most of every brief encounter!

Conclusion

As you have read *Witnessing—A Lifestyle*, my prayer is that it has encouraged, motivated, and equipped you to share your faith with family members, co-workers, neighbors, friends, and those you meet in the community. I hope you've learned that there are many ways to share your faith in your daily life. Lifestyle evangelism involves getting acquainted and helping those you touch to know you care about them!

Let me conclude by encouraging you to begin with small steps like responding to those who ask, "How are you?" with the words, "I'm blessed by God!" And by telling those you know who are going through difficult times, "I will pray for you." Then don't forget to pray and follow up with a telephone call or an e-mail asking how things are going. Let people know you care!

Ask the Lord to open doors of opportunity to share your faith and then wait on Him to open them. Make new friends and enjoy the journey!

I'd love to hear from you! Let me know how you are doing and if we can assist you in any way as you witness in your daily life. May the Lord bless you and your family!

In His Service and yours,

Kay L. Meyer

Family Shield Ministries, Inc.

CHRIST-CENTERED, GOSPEL-FOCUSED, EDUCATIONAL PROGRAMS THAT BUILD STRONG, HEALTHY FAMILIES!

FAMILY LIFE

Nurturing Children within the Home
Families: Yesterday, Today and Tomorrow
Developing a Family Resource Congregation
Families—Tell the Next Generation!
Improving Your Family Life Ministry
Families—Use God's Shield
Fun Family Devotions
Dealing with Fear and Anger
Teaching Your Children Christian Values
Healthy Families Laugh Together
Discipline—God's Way
Six Traits of Healthy Families
Building Family Traditions

SPIRITUAL GROWTH & LEARNING TO WITNESS

Families—Use God's Weapons in the Spiritual Battle
Women of the Bible—Women of Today
Women with New Hearts!
Show Me the Way
Are you Mary or Martha?
Improving Your Prayer Life
Teaching Children to Pray
Using Prayer in Witnessing
Making the Most of Brief Encounters
It's About Life: Physical, Eternal and Abundant Life
Sharing His Promises on Their Level
Motivating Congregational Members to be Organized for Outreach
Responding and Witnessing to Homosexuals
Witnessing—A Lifestyle
Witnessing to Jehovah's Witnesses
Families—Reaching the Lord

To Schedule a Program Call
314-772-6070 or 1-866-370-6070

APPENDIX A—RESOURCES TO HELP YOU GROW

Making Disciples by Donald F. Ginkel (Donald F. Ginkel, 1978)

Share Life—A Witness Workshop, produced by The Lutheran Church—Missouri Synod, Department of Evangelism Ministry.

Re-Turning Church as Home—A Manual for Ministry Among Inactives, produced by The Lutheran Church—Missouri Synod, Department of Evangelism Ministry.

Equipped to Serve, a witness workshop prepared by Lutheran Hour Ministries, 660 Mason Ridge Parkway, St. Louis, MO 63141.

FAMILY SHIELD AUDIO CASSETTES AND CDs FROM THE FAMILY SHIELD RADIO PROGRAM ON WITNESSING
Family Shield is hosted by Kay L. Meyer

Number	Title and Guest
#2	"Witnessing—A Lifestyle" with Dr. A. L. Barry and "What's the Gospel?" with Dr. Dale Meyer.
#101	"Families—Learning to Use God's Shield."
#102	"Fun Family Devotions."
#114	"A Resurrection Quiz for Families."
#118	"Helping Children Learn to Enjoy God's Wonderful World" with Karen Arnold.
#119	"Family and Finances" with Sharon Cleveland.
#124	"Witnessing to Family Members and Friends."
#127	"Witnessing—A Lifestyle" with Dr. A. L. Barry.
#136	"What's the Gospel?" with Dr. Dale Meyer and Roger Hebermehl of Lutheran Hour Ministries.
#144	"Grandparenting—God's Way" with Rev. Roger Sonnenberg and Mrs. William Brauer.
#149	"Sharing Christ with Prisoners and Their Families" with Rev. Paul Beins and Sarah Barnes of Lutheran Ministries.
#150	"Christmas Traditions and Activities for Families."
#151	"Questions Unchurched Ask" with Rev. David Schultz.
#159	"Witness—God's Way."
#163	"Who Is This Jesus?" Part 1, The Humanity of Christ with Rev. Charles Spomer.
#164	"Who Is This Jesus?" Part 2, The Deity of Christ with Rev. Charles Spomer.
#170	"Witnessing to Muslims" with Rev. Ernest Hahn.
#173	"Jewish Evangelism" with Steve Cohen of Apple of His Eye Mission Society.
#174	"What or Who Makes Someone a Christian?" with Professor John Oberdeck of Concordia Seminary.
#182	"Witnessing Effectively to Jehovah's Witnesses" with Kay Meyer. Part one of a five-week series.
#183	"Witnessing Effectively to Jehovah's Witnesses" with Kay Meyer. Part two of a five-week series.
#184	"Witnessing Effectively to Jehovah's Witnesses" with Kay Meyer. Part three of a five-week series.
#185	"Witnessing Effectively to Jehovah's Witnesses" with Kay Meyer. Part four of a five-week series.

#186	"Witnessing Effectively to Jehovah's Witnesses" with Kay Meyer. Part five of a five-week series.
#191	"What Happened to Sin?" with Kevin Meyer and Tim Barrends.
#199	"Children and Worship" with Martha Jander and Rev. Jim Gimbel.
#200	"Peace Officers for Christ International" with Jim Frago and Dave McDowell.
#204	"Making the Most of Your Brief Encounters"
#207	"Witnessing to Policemen and Their Families" with Rev. Steve Lee.
#212	"Responding to the Lodge" with Rev. James Rongstad.
#226	"March for the Real Jesus."
#232	"Infant Baptism" with Professor Tim Saleska and Rev. Ron Rall.
#233	"Infant Baptism vs. Believers Baptism" with Cordell Schulten and Rev. Jeff Gibbs.
#247	"The Law—The Gospel" with Dr. James Kalthoff.
#252	"Christ in the Old Testament" with Professor John Saleska.
#253	"When God Says No" with Carol Henning.
#256	"Persistence in Witnessing" with Rev. and Mrs. Dennis Schmelzer.
#263	"Witnessing to Jehovah's Witnesses" with Jeff Schwehm, a former Jehovah's Witness.
#268	"The Resurrection" with Rev. David V. Schultz.
#270	"Sharing Our Faith" with Rev. Tom Moyer of Ongoing Ambassadors for Christ.
#272-3-4	"Witnessing to Jehovah's Witnesses," Part-One—Part three.
#275	"Families Need the Gospel" with Dr. Lawrence White.
#281	"Families Dealing with Jehovah's Witnesses" with Pat Hallem.
#282	"Exploring Children's Spiritual Development" with Dr. Gary Bertels, Concordia University.
#283	"Prison Ministry" with Jane Otte and Chaplain Michael Carter.
#285	"Nurturing and Sharing Our Faith with Children in the Home."
#290	"Witnessing to Family Members and Friends" with Rev. Roger Sonnenberg.
#293	"Prayer and Witnessing."
#301	"The Incarnation of Christ!" with Rev. David Schultz.
#302	"24 Reasons Jesus Was Born" with Rev. David Schultz.
#307	"No Regrets—How I Got Out of the Mormon Church" with Judy Robertson, Concerned Christians.
#312	"Using God's Weapons Against Satan's Schemes."
#317	"Children's Spiritual Formation" with Dr. Shirley Morganthaler.
#329	"Baptism—What Does the Bible Say?" with Kevin Meyer.
#333	"Witnessing in Families."
#341	"Witnessing to Homosexuals" with Joe Dallas.
#342	"For Faith and Freedom!" With Rev. Paul Devantier.
#351	"Mary Carried Her Cross."
#355	"A Journey of Faith" with Dr. Jeff Schwehm, a former Jehovah's Witness.
#359	"Women Sharing and Witnessing."
#360	"Talking about Jesus with Jehovah's Witnesses."
#364	"Mormonism and Their Temples" with Luke Wilson.
#386	"Why Cult Ministry Is a Family Affair" with Dr. Jeff Schwehm.
#394	"Introduction to Muslims" with Dr. James Dretkee of the Zwemer Institute in Fort Wayne, IN.
#396	"The Incarnation of Christ" with Rev. Ken Wagener.
#397	"Why I Left the Mormon Church" with Melinda Rosenwinkle.
#398	"Jehovah's Witnesses and the Christmas Holidays" with Dr. Jeff Schwehm.
#402	"Out of the Shadows" with Rev. Thomas Lapacka.
#409	"Let's Learn about Witchcraft and Wicca!" with Marcia Montenegro, Christian Answers for the New Age.
#412	"2002 Easter Special."
#415	"Wicca, Witchcraft, and Neopaganism" with Craig Hawkins, author.
#417	"Witnessing—A Lifestyle."
#422	"Fathers as the Spiritual Leader" with David Jander, Mark Dunlop, and William Lubben.
#430	"Jehovah's Witnesses and Its Disfellowshipping and Division of Families" with Dr. Jeff Schwehm.
#431	"Six Traits of Strong Families."
#432	"Understanding My Mormon Friends' Faith and Mine" with Judy Robertson of

Concerned Christians.

#441	"My Hindu Family Disowned Me" with Bansi Brahmbhatt.
#442	"Witnessing to Families" with Rev. Dave Mulder.
#452	"Show Me the Way!"
#459	"Witnessing to Gypsies" with Rev. Larry Merino.
#460	"Jehovah's Witnesses and End Times" – Part I with Dr. Jeff Schwehm.
#461	"Jehovah's Witnesses and End Times"—Part II with Dr. Jeff Schwehm.
#464	"Reaching Unchurched Families Through Christian Schools and the St. Louis Metro Voice" with Jim Day.
#472	"Improving Your Congregation's Outreach Efforts" Part I with Kay Meyer.
#474	"Improving Your Congregation's Outreach Efforts" Part II with Kay Meyer.
#478	"Devotions for Children."
#492	"Reaching Families for Christ" with Kay Meyer and Rev. Timothy Knapp.
#500	"Sharing Christ During the Holidays."
#506	"Jehovah's Witnesses and Shunning" with Dr. Jeff Schwehm. Includes calls from four former Witnesses who have been shunned.
#510	"The Challenges of the Cults" with Ron Rhodes, author.
#516	"Three Days—Three Nights" with Tim Hetzner, Lutheran Church Charities.
#528	"L.A.M.P." with Rev. Don Johnson.
#534	"Biblical Illiteracy" with Tim Hetzner, Lutheran Church Charities.
#545	"A Jewish Businessman Encounters the Living Christ" with Stan Telchin of Jews for Jesus.
#547	"The Incarnation of Christ" with Rev. Mark Smith of Prince of Peace Lutheran Church.
#556	"Celebrations, Milestones, and Family Ministry" with Jill Hasstedt and Krista Young.
#557	"When Homosexuality Hits Home" with Joe Dallas. Underwritten by First Light.
#574	"Responding to Wicca" with Marcia Montenagra of CANA.
#586	"Witnessing to Strangers" with Rev. David Bueltmann, President, CID District.
#589	"Witnessing to Jehovah's Witnesses" with Dr. Jeff Schwehm.
#590	"Witnessing to Jehovah's Witnesses" with Kay Meyer.
#595	"Telling the Old, Old Story of Christ's Birth" with Timothy Hetzner, President, Lutheran Church Charities.
#598	"Teaching Children to Pray."
#600	"Spiritual Warfare and Today's Families" with Rev. Jerry Kosberg.
#601	"Special Children Bring Special Gifts" with Karen and Miki Cunningham and Chuck Conover.
#602	"Witnessing in Rural Communities" with Rev. Gaylord Spilker.
#603	"Witnessing to Jewish Friends" with Rev. Edward Balfour.
#604	"Won Out of Lesbianism" with Melissa Fryrear of Focus on the Family.
#607	"Witnessing—A Lifestyle" with Rev. Scott Snow.
#609	"How Christian Radio Impacted Our Life!" With Ken Tobler and Pat Hallem.
#615	"St. John's Outpost Maplewood" with Jim Britton and Ryan Peterson.
#617	"Christ Memorial Moves to Target" with Rev. Jeff Cloeter, Chris Wilson.
#622	"Witnessing to Your Doctor" with Dr. William Schuh.
#623	"Responding to Atheists, Agnostics and Skeptics" with Ron Rhodes.
#624	"Reaching the Unchurched" with Kevin Rudd.
#634	"Lawyers Witnessing to Lawyers" with Cordell Schulten.
#635	"Engaging the Secular World with a Spiritual Message" with Rev. Steven Siegel.
#637	"Shining the Light into the Darkness" with Rev. Phil Pledger of Lutheran Braille Workers.
#638	"Responding in Love to Mormons" with Bill McKeever, Morman Research Ministry with Host Roland Lettner.
#639	"Spellbound" with Marcia Montengra.
#649	"Responding in Love to Muslims."
#652	"Tell the Next Generation" with Dr. Dick Hardel.
#658	"Witness—A Lifestyle" with David Vaughn and Tim Hetzner.
#662	"Christians Ablaze!" with Dr. Gerald Kieschnick, President, the LCMS.
#664	"Homosexuals and God's Grace" with Joe Dallas.
#674	"What Do Mormons Believe About God?" With Bill McKeever of Mormon Research Ministry.

#675	"Lutheran Association of Missionaries and Pilots—Reaching Native Americans" with Dr. Don Johnson and Will and Patricia Main.
#677	"Responding and Witnessing to Jehovah's Witnesses" with Kay Meyer. Roland Lettner: Host.
#678	"How to Help Families Address Crisis and Stress" with Dr. Mark Hannemann and Kristen Ruttencutter.
#681	"Enter Through the Narrow Gate" with Rev. Ron Rall.
#682	"Dealing with Conflict in the Workplace" with Ted Kober.
#684	"Learning to Pray" with Rev. Craig Otto.
#686	"Growing Leaders" with Rev. Steve Wagner.
#690	"Stories That Touch Your Heart."
#692	"Traditions and the Holidays."

To order, send the form below with a check for $6 for audiocassettes and $8 for CD's to:

Family Shield Ministries, Inc.

P. O. Box 230015

St. Louis, MO 63123

AUDIOCASSETTE AND CD ORDER FORM: Please send tape # _____. _____,

_____, _____. Circle "AUDIOCASSETTE" or "CD" on the line above to indicate your choice.

NAME _____ ORGANIZATION _____

ADDRESS_____ CITY _____ STATE _____ ZIP_____

TELEPHONE _____

You may also call to charge your resource at 1-866-370-6070.

*** Postage and handling included.

WEBSITES

www.familyshieldministries.com

www.focusonthefamily.org

www.youthandfamilyinstitute.org

www.lhm.org

www.lcms.org

www.peacemakerministries.com

www.georgebarna.org

www.evangelism.com

www.evantell.org

www.christiananswers.net

www.missionevangelism.org

www.evangelismresources.org

www.globalrecordings.net

www.shareyourfaith.org

www.campuscrusadeforchrist.com

APPENDIX B—BIBLE VERSES RELATED TO WITNESSING

The Great Commission

"I have been given all authority in heaven and earth, Go, then, to all people everywhere and make them my disciples, baptize them in the name of the Father, the Son, and the Holy Spirit, and teach them to obey all I commanded you. And I will be with you always, to the end of the age" (Matthew 28:18-20, GNB).

Where does the power come from?

"But you will receive power when the Holy Spirit has come upon you; and you shall be my witnesses both in Jerusalem, and in all Judea and Samaria, and even to the remotest part of the earth" (Acts 1:8).

What will I say?

"But when they hand you over, do not worry about how or what you are to say; for it will be given you in that hour what you are to say. For it is not you who speak, but it is the Spirit of your Father who speaks in you" (Matthew 10:19-20).

Keeping the Law can't save you

"Because by the works of the Law no flesh will be justified in His sight; for through the Law comes the knowledge of sin" (Romans 3:20).

All of us are sinners

"For all have sinned and fall short of the glory of God, being justified as a gift by His grace through the redemption which is in Christ Jesus" (Romans 3:23-24).

You are saved by faith, not works!

"For by grace you have been saved through faith; and that not of yourselves, it is the gift of God; not as a result of your works, so that no one may boast" (Ephesians 2:8-9).

Believe in Jesus as your Savior

"For God so loved the world, that He gave His only begotten Son, that whoever believes in Him shall not perish, but have eternal life" (John 3:16).

God's Word is inspired and equips us

"All Scripture is inspired by God and profitable for teaching, for reproof, for correction, for training in righteousness; so that the man of God may be adequate, equipped for every good work" (2 Timothy 3:16-17).

This is the Gospel!

"Now I make known to you, brethren, the gospel which I preached to you, which also you received, in which also you stand, by which also you are saved, if you hold fast the word which I preached to you, unless you believed in vain. For I delivered to you as of first importance what I also received, that Christ died for our sins according to the Scriptures [the Old Testament—Isaiah 53:5-12], and that He was buried, and that He was raised on the third day according to the Scriptures [Psalm 16:8], and that He appeared to Cephas [Peter], then to the twelve. After that He appeared to more than five hundred brethren at one time, most of whom remain until now, but some have fallen asleep; then He appeared to James, then to all the apostles, and last of all, as to one untimely born, He appeared to me also" (1 Corinthians 15:1-7).

Peter preaches: "Repent and be baptized!"

"And they were filled with the Holy Spirit and began to speak with other tongues, as the Spirit was giving them utterance. 'This Man, delivered over by the predetermined plan and foreknowledge of God, you nailed to a cross by the hands of godless men and put Him to death. And God raised Him up again, putting an end to the agony of death, since it was impossible for Him to be held in its power.' Now when they heard this, they were pierced to the heart, and said to Peter and the rest of the apostles, 'Brethren, what shall we do?' And Peter said to them, 'Repent, and each of you be baptized in the name of Jesus Christ for the forgiveness of your sins; and you will receive the gift of the Holy Spirit. For the promise is for you and for your children, and for all who are far off, as many as the Lord our God will call to Himself'" (Acts. 2:3, 23-24, 37-39).

Paul and Silas witness to prisoners and jailers

"But about midnight Paul and Silas were praying and singing hymns of praise to God, and the prisoners were listening to them; and suddenly there came a great earthquake, so that the foundations of the prison house were shaken; and immediately all the doors were opened and everyone's chains were unfastened..." (Acts 16:25-26).

The jailer asks, "What must I do to be saved?"

"And after he brought them out, he said, 'Sirs, what must I do be saved?' They said, 'Believe in the Lord Jesus, and you shall be saved, you and your household.' And they spoke the word of the Lord to him together with all who were in his house. And he took them that very hour of the night and washed their wounds, and immediately he was baptized, he and all his household" (Acts 16: 30-33).

Philip shares Christ with the Ethiopian

"But an angel of the Lord spoke to Philip saying, 'Get up and go south to the road that descends from Jerusalem to Gaza.'... So he got up and went; and there was an Ethiopian eunuch, a court official of Candace, queen of the Ethiopians, who was in charge of all her treasure; and he had come to Jerusalem to worship, ... Philip ran up and heard him reading Isaiah the prophet, and said, 'Do you understand what you are reading?' And he said, 'Well, how could I, unless someone guides me?' And he invited Philip to come up and sit with him. ... Then Philip opened his mouth, and beginning from this Scripture he preached Jesus to him. As they went along the road they came to some water; and the eunuch said, 'Look! Water! What prevents me from being baptized?' [And Philip said, 'If you believe with all your heart, you may.' And he answered and said, 'I believe that Jesus Christ is the Son of God']" (Acts 8:26-27, 30-31, 35-37).

John proclaims the Word of Life

"What was from the beginning, what we have heard, what we have seen with our eyes, what we looked at and touched with our hands, concerning the Word of Life—and the life was manifested, and we have seen and testify and proclaim to you the eternal life, which was with the Father and was manifested to us..." (1 John 1:1-2)

Always be ready to make a defense to everyone who asks

"...but sanctify Christ as Lord in your hearts, always being ready to make a defense to everyone who asks you to give an account for the hope that is in you, yet with gentleness and reverence" (1 Peter 3:15).

APPENDIX C—SO YOU'RE THE LEADER OF THE WITNESSING—A LIFESTYLE DISCUSSION GROUP

Although many who receive this book will read it, the Board of Directors and I envision that some Christians will decide it will be beneficial to gather friends from their congregation or church group to discuss various chapters together. Congregational leaders might also read a chapter at a Board of Education or Board of Evangelism meeting and discuss what they learn together. Being the leader is a wonderful privilege, but sometimes can be overwhelming. The following are some suggestions for leaders to consider:

1. Begin your preparation and planning with prayer. Ask the Lord for His wisdom as you read, study, digest and prepare to lead group discussions, devotions, and/or Bible studies. Pray that you are sensitive to each person's needs. Remember some people will be feeling guilt over not witnessing in the past.

2. Read the section or chapter to be discussed in advance. Study the Bible verses in it. Write out the Bible verses and answers to questions that are asked or that come to your mind as you read.

3. Be open and honest with other participants about your struggles in applying faith to life and witnessing. Be prepared to share examples, but don't monopolize the conversation.

4. Don't feel that you must answer every question or discuss every Bible verse. Don't get sidetracked on questions from participants that don't relate to the topic. Stick to the topic.

5. Set a specific time to start and end. Make sure you begin and end on time.

6. Begin and end each session with prayer.

7. Encourage individuals that attend to read the segment or chapter that will be discussed in advance. Another alternative is to read the chapter silently or aloud as you begin the session. Then discuss one or more of the following paragraphs with your group:

APPENDIX D—DISCUSSION GROUP QUESTIONS

Part One—Witnessing Basics

1. Witnessing Basics has several chapters that focus on prayer and its importance in the witnessing process. Why is prayer so important to this process? Why should we be specific in our prayer requests? As you read this segment the Lord probably brought someone to mind that you could pray for who is unsaved. If appropriate, share with the group who that is and why you think prayer is important. Invite them to keep this person in their prayers.

2. What does it mean to go ahead of the Holy Spirit? Have you ever done this? What happened? Why is it better to wait on the Lord to open doors? How do you know when the Lord is opening a door to witness? How can questions be used in sharing our faith with family and friends?

3. Why is listening attentively important in effective witnessing? What can you learn when you listen? Why is knowing about their family, work, interest, and hobbies helpful? Have you ever had someone ask you a question about God, the church, or His Word that opened up a spiritual conversation? Share what happened with the group.

4. What are the seven key points to share when introducing someone to Christ? Talk about each point individually and how you might use this as you witness. Discuss the Bible verses related to each point. Why would listening attentively help you know what the person needs to hear? Why is it important that those we are talking to understand they cannot do good works to be saved? Why do you think so many people think they have to do something to please God? Participants might consider memorizing each of the seven key points.

5. What are the four obstacles to prayer? Review the Bible verses that talk about these obstacles together. Have you ever seen any of these obstacles in your life or in someone's that you know? Share an example with your group. How might knowing these obstacles help you witness to someone who says, "God doesn't answer my prayers!"

6. What did you learn about congregational prayer ministries and prayer chains? Does your congregation have a prayer chain? How might the information in this chapter help you get one started or expand your program?

Part Two—Witnessing Begins at Home

1. Why do you think that the church needs to partner with the home in helping build strong, healthy families? How is your congregation doing this?

2. Twenty-five years of research has shown that there are six-characteristics or traits that build strong, healthy families. They include: commitment to promoting each other's welfare and happiness, appreciation and affection, positive communication, time together, spiritual well-being, and the ability to cope with stress and crises. Talk about each characteristic and the Bible verses that relate to them. How is your family doing? Which of the six traits do you need to focus on? How might your church help you and other families?

3. How did you come to know Jesus as your Savior and Lord? Who impacted your spiritual life the most? How many of you came to faith because a family member brought you to be baptized or told you about Jesus? How do you share your faith at home and with your extended family? Why is forgiveness a necessary ingredient in every family? How do you share forgiveness in your family? With children? Your spouse? Your grandchildren? Your extended family?

4. This section also talks about spiritual warfare and Satan's schemes. What were some of the schemes that were discussed? How do you resist Satan's schemes? Go through the list of nine ways we can resist Satan's schemes. Look up, read, and discuss the Bible verse that accompanies each one. Pray that the Lord would give you strength to continue to stand firm in the faith and shield your families from false teachings and dangerous practices.

5. Read "Everyday Missionaries Share the Good News!" silently or aloud. Then discuss each bolded section together.

Part Three—Witness During Holidays

1. What is your favorite holiday memory from your childhood? Why do you think memories are important?

2. This section shared ways to share your faith during Halloween, Thanksgiving, Christmas, Easter, and several other holidays. Share one idea

from the book that you think you could implement in your family, school, or congregation. Depending upon the time of year, discuss one of the holidays and the suggestions that were in the chapter with your group. What does your family do that those in your group might want to know about?

3. If you have extended family members who are unchurched or who are not Christians, take time at the close of the session to pray for that person by name. Ask others to also pray for him/her.

Part Four—Witness in the Community, Congregations and Schools

1. Read "Sharing the Gospel" together. Ask those present to define the Gospel. Ask them to consider doing an informal survey and ask five friends, neighbors, or co-workers over the next week what they think the word Gospel means. Tell them not to debate their answers, but just write down what they say and share it with you the following week. Was there confusion? One of the most common issues is that people believe that they are saved because they are good people and that they can earn God's favor and eternal life. Discuss how to lovingly address this issue with someone they know.

2. Read "Engaging the Secular World in Spiritual Conversations." Discuss Steve Siegel's comment toward the end where he said, "Kay, I could have closed down the discussion numerous times. I could have raised barriers by becoming angry that she had compared me to a 1920s gangster. I didn't. I just laughed when she made that comparison. I could have been judgmental and criticized her for selecting a fiancé who was an illegal immigrant or said something negative about her working in Las Vegas. Again, I didn't." In your closing prayer ask the Lord to open up opportunities for you to witness this week.

3. Read "Making the Most of Brief Encounters." How did Jesus, the apostles, and disciples use brief encounters to share their faith? Look up some of the Bible verses about brief encounters. Read and discuss a few of them together. Can you think of other brief encounters from God's Word? Share a time when God opened up a brief encounter for you. What happened? What might you do differently next time?

4. Read "Proclaim the Law—Then Share the Gospel" silently or together. Sometimes we speak to unbelievers or unsaved people as if they are

Christians and what we say is over their heads theologically. Would we try to teach division to a child who can't yet add or subtract? Then why do we try to talk to those who do not know Christ, as if they do? Stick with the basics when speaking to those who do not know Christ! What happens when we talk to people about things they do not understand?

5. Talking about sin isn't easy in today's world. Why is the law and Gospel necessary when witnessing to someone who does not know Christ? How could you bring up the topic of sin when speaking to family members and friends?

APPENDIX E—DISCUSSION STARTERS FOR WITNESSING IN YOUR EVERYDAY LIFE

Select one of the situations below and discuss with your small group.

1) You are flying home from a trip by yourself and strike up a conversation with a young mother sitting next to you. She tells you she is returning home after seeing her father who recently suffered a heart attack. As you talk you discover she does not attend church. She has no background in the church. When she finds out you are a Christian she asks, "Do you really believe people go to heaven when they die?" How would you respond?

2) A Jewish co-worker enjoys your company and asks if you would like to take a walk with her on your breaks. You have been praying for her for over a year. You decide this is an open door from the Lord for sharing your faith. As you begin walking each day with her, what would you do and say to begin to share your faith with her in a non-threatening way?

3) Your eight-year-old son brings home a new friend who recently moved into your community. He asked if the friend can join you for dinner. During family devotions you discover that this boy does not attend Sunday school or church. What can you do to share Christ with him? With his parents?

4) You learn that a friend's husband is very ill. This couple used to attend your church, but doesn't attend anymore. You have been praying for them. How can you share the love of Christ with them?

5) You see a couple that you don't know standing outside of church. As you begin talking with them you discover they recently moved to the city and are Baptist. They tell you they really enjoyed the service. Then they ask you to explain why Lutherans baptize infants. They really seem interested and explain that they just learned that they are going to have a baby. What do you say? Do?

6) Your sister grew up attending church, but hasn't attended for several years. She is divorced. Her teenager is causing her grief. She asks for your help and assistance. What do you say? How can you witness to her in a non-threatening way?

7) Your father, who only attends church a few times a year, has never spoken of his love for Christ to you. You are not certain that he even believes in God. He suffers a heart attack and you learn that he only has a few months to live. When you visit him, what do you say? How could you witness in non-threatening ways?

8) You and your husband invite a couple that recently moved in next-door over for cake and coffee. You want to get to know them better. You know they are not Christians or at least that they do not attend church. How might you eventually witness to them?

9) Your 14-year-old daughter tells you she doesn't want to attend church anymore. She says it's boring. What do you say?

10) At lunch with a business acquaintance who attends a different denomination, you discover that he believes he is going to heaven because he has been a good person. Would you respond at this time? If so, what would you say? If not, what might you do later?

11) You lose your temper at work and say things to your secretary that you are sorry for afterward. You ask God to forgive you. Now you must ask your secretary to forgive you, too. How can you use this situation to witness for Christ?

12) Discussing religion with a co-worker at dinner she responds, "All religions are the same, aren't they? What difference does it make if I attend church? Sundays are my only day to sleep in. I work hard during the week. I'm sure God understands." Read and discuss Hebrews 10:23-25 in light of these comments. Are all religions the same? How is Christianity different?

13) A co-worker states, "I don't believe that people are sinful from birth. I guess I don't believe in original sin." How would you respond?

APPENDIX F—ABOUT THE AUTHOR

Kay L. Meyer is the founder and president of Family Shield Ministries, Inc. and host of its weekly, hour-long *Family Shield* radio program. She has over 25 years experience in evangelism, education, and family ministry. Meyer is a frequent consultant, speaker and author on family life, prayer, spiritual growth, apologetics, and learning to witness. Sample publications include: *Family Ministry Basics* (CPH, 2006); *Mission Field on Our Doorstep: Jehovah's Witnesses* (Family Shield, 2004); *Teaching Your Children Christian Values* (CPH, 1996); *Life in the Sandwich Generation* (CPH, 1995); and contributions to *Portals of Prayer, Teachers Interaction,* and *My Devotions.* Meyer has also written "The Great Commission" for the *St. Louis Metro Voice* newspaper since 1994. The column helps Christians learn how to share their faith in their daily life.

Meyer has a Master of Arts in Media Communications from Webster University, St. Louis, and a Bachelor of Science in Education. She and her husband, Tjaden (Chad) Meyer, have been married over 40 years. They have three grown children and three grandchildren. The Meyers are members of Concordia Lutheran Church in Kirkwood, Missouri, and associate members of Christ in the City Lutheran Church.

APPENDIX G—
ABOUT FAMILY SHIELD MINISTRIES, INC.

Do you know that 125 million people in the United States do not know Christ as their Savior and Lord? Or that the United States is one of the largest mission fields in the world? *"The harvest is plentiful, but the workers are few. Therefore beseech the Lord of the harvest to send out workers into His harvest" (Matthew 9:37-38).*

Family Shield Ministries, Inc., a Recognized Service Organization of The Lutheran Church—Missouri Synod, is dedicated to reaching and equipping individuals and their families for Christ. The organization is self-supporting and self-governing. It receives donations and financial support from 1,300 individuals, families, congregations, and organizations in 33 states. Family Shield has numerous ministries that reach beyond the walls of the church. One of them is its Family Shield radio program that is currently heard in nine states throughout the Midwest.

THE MISSION
To educate and equip people, through the power of the Gospel, to know Christ, grow in His Word, and strengthen individuals and their families.

"Taking up the shield of faith with which you will be able to extinguish all the flaming arrows of the evil one" (Ephesians 6:16).

GOALS

1) To share the Gospel with those who do not know Christ and those who are unchurched.
2) To equip Christians to apply faith to life, motivate them to grow in faith and in the knowledge of God's Word so they can discern truth from error, and use their gifts to serve and witness in the home, community, and church.
3) To connect people with needs to resources.
4) To develop partnerships and collaborations with Christian organizations and congregations.
5) To help individuals and families implement the six traits for healthy families.

PARTNER ORGANIZATIONS

Lutheran Hour Ministries
LCMS World Missions—Ablaze!®
Lutheran Church Charities of Chicago
Holy Cross Lutheran Church, St. Louis, Missouri
Ascension Lutheran Church, St. Louis, Missouri

MINISTRIES, PROGRAMS, AND SERVICES

- *Family Shield,* a weekly Gospel-centered radio program broadcast on 11 stations in nine states.
- The Response Center, coordinated for us by Lutheran Hour Ministries through a partnership, receives telephone calls and sends complimentary booklets and resources.
- Cult Ministry, specializing in sharing the Gospel with Jehovah's Witnesses, others caught in the false teachings of cults and/or the occult, and assisting family members and friends.
- "The Great Commission" is a newspaper column written by Kay L. Meyer in the *St. Louis Metro Voice* newspaper.
- Bible-based educational programs on family life, parenting, apologetics, prayer, spiritual growth, and learning to witness.
- Evangelism and Family Ministry Services

To schedule a program, learn about services, or find out how you can support the ministry, contact (314) 772-6070 or (866) 370-6070. To receive a complimentary booklet on a wide range of family life topics, call the Response Center at (877) 317-4326. You can also write to the address below or visit www.familyshieldministries.com.

P. O. Box 230015
St. Louis, MO 63123
(314) 772-6070 (866) 370-6070
www.familyshieldministries.com

APPENDIX H—STORIES OF THOSE WE TOUCHED

Each year the ministry gets telephone calls, e-mails and letters from thousands of individuals struggling with a problem or wanting to learn more about God's Word and witnessing. Some are Christians, many are not. Here are a few examples of the people we reach and equip through the ministries.

"I have always been reluctant to talk about my faith, but after attending Family Shield's six-week seminar on 'Witnessing—A Lifestyle,' I was able to share my faith with my unchurched neighbor. Thank you for giving me the ability and courage to share Christ with my family and friends!" Karen

"I was always afraid to speak up for Christ, but after reading your witnessing column for the past few years, I began praying that God would help me talk to family and friends about my Savior. Yesterday God opened a door for me to talk about Jesus with a co-worker. He gave me the words in the hour that I needed them. Thank you for your column!" Scott

"Thank you for presenting the six-week series to the Concordia Seminary wives this year. I learned so much about sharing my faith with my children and those in my family!"

"Our next door neighbor doesn't attend church. Yesterday she asked if I knew of an organization that could help her. She recently got a divorce and is dealing with a lot of anger. Is there a Christian divorce recovery group that we could recommend?" We referred this caller to a Christian divorce recovery organization and sent her a copy of a program we produced that featured this organization. We also included an audiocassette from another program on "Dealing with Anger Biblically."

"Thank you for presenting 'Setting Boundaries for Children' at the parenting class last week at Hope Lutheran Church. I could tell from the discussion that the parents gained valuable insights into how to set boundaries in the home. After the class one mother told me, 'I can't wait to get home to implement some of the suggestions that were shared today.' I appreciate the fact that you related faith to daily life and helped parents realize that forgiveness is a necessary ingredient in healthy families."

Shana wrote, "Thank you for your prayers for me and my son, believing in me, even when I didn't believe in myself. Thank you for teaching me about parenting and about the Lord. I knew you would be glad to hear that I finished my undergraduate degree last year. My son and I are doing well. I just wanted to say thank you! You will never know how much your interest and support meant to me."

"I wanted to let you and your prayer partners know how my husband and I are doing. When we first spoke after I heard the Family Shield program entitled 'Building Healthy Marriages' my husband and I were discussing a separation. Thank you for praying with me and recommending that we see a Christian counselor. We are seeing a great counselor and addressing our marital problems." Michelle

"Thought you might like to know that I came to faith through Christian radio. I continue to listen because programs like yours encourage and equip me in my walk with Christ. *Family Shield* is making an eternal difference in the lives of thousands of people." Ken

"I just wanted to call and tell you how much we appreciate your prayers for my husband who has been unemployed. He has two interviews that sound promising this week. Please continue your prayers." Lorena

APPENDIX I—WHAT OTHERS SAY ABOUT FAMILY SHIELD MINISTRIES

The success of Family Shield Ministries is a result of a vital need in the community. It is a family-oriented ministry that equips individuals and families to deal with problems through God's Word. It is a ministry that encourages people to be strong in their faith and to resist Satan's schemes. And, most importantly, a ministry that provides solid instruction on how to reach out to family members, friends, and neighbors with the saving Gospel of Jesus Christ. This ministry is focused on "encouraging," "equipping," and "spreading the Good News." It is truly unique and deserves our support.

Jim Day, Publisher
The St. Louis Metro Voice

Listen to *FAMILY SHIELD*

Hosted by Kay L. Meyer

Family Shield is a weekly, hour-long radio program that is heard in 9 states. It addresses family life, apologetics and spiritual growth.

AM 850 KFUO—St. Louis
11:05 a.m. on Saturday
7:05 p.m. on Sunday
www.kfuo.org

WCGR FM 89.5—Chicago
7:00 p.m. on Wednesday
www.cuchicago.edu/multimedia/wcgn

KCCV AM 760— Kansas City
3:00 p.m. on Saturday
www.bottradionetwork.com

WLUJ FM 89.7—Springfield, IL
and affiliates that include:
88.1 FM Petersburg, 88.3 FM White Hall, 100.1 FM Decatur, 100.1 FM Lincoln, and 93.5 FM Jacksonville
12 noon on Sunday
www.wluj.com

KNGN AM 1360— McCook, NE
3:00 p.m. on Sundays
www.kngn.org

WGVE FM 88.7—Gary, IN
1:00 a.m. on Saturday & Sunday
www.wgve887fm.org

Family Shield Ministries, Inc.
www.familyshieldministries.com,
familyshield@familyshieldministries.com
1-314-772-6070 or 1-866-370-6070.

Support Family Shield Ministries, Inc.

Yes! Our family, group, congregation, or business would like to make a donation to Family Shield. ❑ Where most needed.... or ❑ To the Family Shield radio program in: ❑ St. Louis ❑ Chicago ❑ Kansas City ❑ Springfield, IL ❑ New Markets

Enclosed is a ❑ One time ❑ Monthly ❑ Quarterly gift of: ❑ $500 ❑ $250 ❑ $100 ❑ $50 ❑ $_____. Total pledge amount $_____.

Name _____

Organization_____

Address _____

City/State/Zip _____

Telephone _____

E-mail _____

Three Ways to Give:

1) By check: Please make payable to Family Shield Ministries and mail to P. O. Box 230015, St. Louis, MO 63123.

2) By credit card: Charge your gift by filling out the information below or by calling us toll free at 1 (866) 370-6070. ❑ Master Card ❑ Visa ❑ Amount $_____

Credit Card #_____

Expiration Date _____

_____

Signature (sign here to authorize your pledge and payment method)

_____

Please print name as it appears on card.

3) Online: Donate a gift at www.familyshieldministries.com. Click the **Donate Now** button under "Support Information." Then follow the directions.

DONATE NOW THROUGH
Network for **Good**

Thrivent Match: Are you a Thrivent member? ___Yes ___ No

Chapter Name:_____

Please copy this page as needed. More information on next page.

Christian Stewardship:

Yes! I would like to know more about Christian stewardship. Have a representative call me to set up an appointment to discuss:

☐ Gift Annuities   ☐ Will or Living Trust

☐ Charitable Remainder Trust   ☐ Life Insurance Policy

☐ Gifts of Cash or Securities   ☐ Donating Real Estate

Please send me information about:

☐ How we can get your radio program in our community

☐ Family Life Seminars

☐ Learning to Witness Seminars

☐ The Cult/Occult Ministry

☐ Resources for those who are unchurched

Please send the Family Shield E-mail newsletter to me:

E-mail: _____

Good News For Life!

Lutherans For Life exists to help Christ's people understand that life issues are spiritual issues to which the Gospel of Jesus Christ speaks.

We exist to encourage and equip Christ's people to help others make this connection.

God's Word changes hearts and minds.

God's Word changes people's lives who are struggling with these issues.

We invite you to make use of our resources to share the most powerful and positive pro-life message in the universe—the Gospel of Jesus!

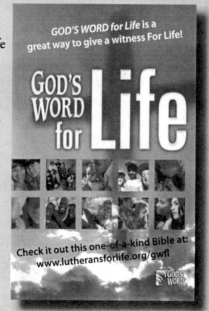

GOD'S WORD for Life is a great way to give a witness For Life!

GOD'S WORD for Life

Check it out this one-of-a-kind Bible at:
www.lutheransforlife.org/gwfl

GOD'S WORD

Lutherans For Life • 888-364-LIFE • www.lutheransforlife.org

YOU have a mission

Ablaze!

www.lcms.org/ablaze
LCMS WORLD MISSION

in your home, neighborhood, nation, and world

LCMS World Mission
is your link to mission action...

Visit www.lcms.org.ablaze or call 1-800-433-3954

Read faith-sharing stories from LCMS
members and share your own.

Access outreach resources, tool, and tips.

Learn about global missionary service.
Serve anywhere from 2 weeks to 2 years.

LCMS WORLD MISSION
The Global Gospel Outreach of The Lutheran Church–Missouri Synod
www.lcmsworldmission.org

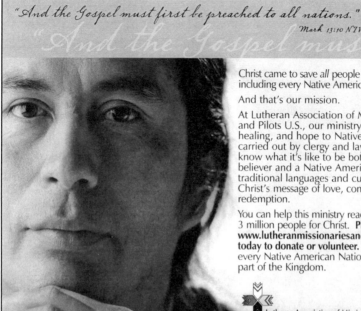

Family Shield Ministries, Inc.

Witnessing—A Lifestyle
Seminar

Your congregation, zone, or circuit can sponsor a Family Shield "Witnessing—A Lifestyle" seminar. The seminar equips Christians to witness in their daily lives to family, friends, co-workers, and those in their community.

What participants have said:

"During the seminar I learned how to open up conversations related to faith in a natural gentle way. The week after the training God opened a door for me to share my faith with a friend. Thank you for sharing this important information and helping me share the Gospel!" Marsha

"I have always been reluctant to talk about my faith, but after attending the six-week seminar on 'Witnessing—A Lifestyle,' I was able to share my faith with my neighbor. Thank you for giving me the ability and courage to share Christ with my family and friends!" Ben

To Schedule a Seminar
(or to order more copies of this book)
call
314-772-6070 or 1-866-370-6070

NOTES

NOTES